MW00649532

# From the Attic

# to the Altar

Unless otherwise indicated, all Scripture quotations are taken from the *King James Verion* of the Bible.

*From the Attic to the Altar*
Copyright © 2003
Antoinette Mann
ISBN 0-88144-000-0

Published by Christian Publishing Services, Inc.
2448 East 81st Street, Suite 4550
Tulsa, OK 74137

Editorial Consultant: Cory Emerson
Cover Art: Whisner Design Group
Text Design: Lisa Simpson

Printed in the United States of America.
toni@resoundmedia.com

# Contents

# Dedication

Dedicated to my Dad, Harold Lewis Sr., who left to be with the Lord three weeks before this book was complete. Had he not saved me from a life of abandonment in an attic and taught me with a love only the Heavenly Father above could have given him for me, I truly would not know where I am going.

# *Acknowledgement*

Ginni Hall did exceedingly and abundantly above all to help me put my story in print. We met in 1993 in my Christian bookstore "A Sign of the Dove." I had written the first four chapters of my book and had stopped because my life was falling apart one more time, and I could not put in writing the hurt in my heart. I was writing the story then using a recorder to speak what I had written so a local firm there could transcribe it. Ginni was a transcriber also, so I began to give her my tapes. Punctuation and spelling have never been my forte, so we were a good fit. It put a fire under me to have a friend that could see my hurt. When I left my reader in the dark, she would pull the rest of the story out of the recesses of my mind. Then I began to see what a mess my life was in print and I hit a wall. Knowing that Ginni was also a writer, I asked her if she would ghostwrite a fiction story around my story, which she did. She dreamed up the characters and the fictitious city they lived in and I was Jocelyn Hope, the heroine you just couldn't help but love. All I can say is I got a wonderful healing and some holy boldness out of that fiction. Now I asked Ginni if we could go back to our original plan as I felt the Lord wanted my story to be real.

This is not my life story, but these are the true stories from my life. Ginni has seen my heart like no other, and has pushed me through. I know she has lived parts of my story, and this has been another reason she has been there for me so many times. My favorite saying fits her and me so well. GOD NEVER PUTS ONE ON ONE FOR ONE–HE ALWAYS DOES A WORK IN BOTH.

I also wish to acknowledge my sons, Joseph and Bryan, who have made my life so exciting with their adventures added to mine. Although my time with my son, Steven, was much shorter than I would have wished, he taught me about unconditional love and how to be an overcomer.

There are many other people who encouraged me along the way, especially my husband, Rick, my granddaughter, Aryn Brianna, and my adopted daughter, Lisa Lane. Other supportive friends were Rabbi David and Bobbie Barsky, Bill and Sherry Heilig, Jim and Barb Hickey, Irvin and Joanna Hicks, Bea Kassee, Steve and Jody Richmond, Johnny and Janet Wagoner. Last, but not least, my beloved brother, Harold Jr., and my sis, Demona.

The author would like to acknowledge the professional editing services provided by Cory Emberson of Lightspeed Editing, 20511 Skywest Drive, Hayward, CA 94541.

# *Preface*

Perhaps you are asking yourself why I wrote this particular book. You may be assured that it is certainly not because I feel that I am a great writer. Nor do I believe that my story is any more important than the hundreds or thousands of other stories that could have been written by people who have been through some very similar experiences. No. The purpose of this book is very different. I'm just an ordinary person who has had some very difficult and trying experiences; but I've also had more than my share of triumphs, glorious victories, and heaven-sent miracles.

I want to reach my hand out to those of you who are either in one of those dark cave experiences right now, or have endured so much pain and suffering in your life that you may have even wanted to die. But please let me encourage you, for there is a **Great Hope**. Listen to me when I tell you that I have walked similar paths to those you may find yourself walking. I have stumbled and fallen many times; my body has ached for comfort and my face was constantly wet with tears, but the Lord was and is and always will be there, for you as well as for me.

Now as you read these stories, let me show you how He has been there in each and every one. Sometimes the presence and provision of God is so obvious in what happens that everyone can see it; but in some situations, God is perhaps just a mere whisper of hope into the ear of a desperate child. It is my sincere desire and it would be my great joy, if, as you read this book, you will see Him, both in His Glory and in His simplicity, and relate it to your own experience. Reflect on how He has been there in the past and watch eagerly for His hand in

9

your future, because He says He will never leave us nor forsake us.

Once you acknowledge His presence and accept your trials as battles against your enemy, Satan, God will help you fight those battles. As a matter of fact, He will fight in your place if you learn to step back and let Him. You see, the fight is God over evil, good over bad. You must listen and hear what He says, then do it with all your heart. If God is who you are following, after that circumstance in your life is over, you can know your life will be richer, deeper, filled with joy and all the things He promises His children. He is developing your character if you will but let Him. Then you will no longer be a victim. At that point, the Light of Truth and the God of Heaven will lead you out of that dark cave if, in your heart of hearts, you really want out. The secret is that you have to be willing to do it **His** way. I promise you, it will be much better than anything you could ever imagine. He tells us that His ways are higher than our ways.

I also want you to understand that the Father often does simple, unexpected things for His children, as well. In fact, let's take a little imaginary side trip here, and I'll show you what I mean. Picture a child on the way home from school. She's kicking the rocks in her path and shuffling along in a rather despondent mood. She knows what's waiting. As she trudges up the steps to her front porch, she can still hear her mother's voice from that morning.

"I need your room cleaned by tonight. We're having company, and it's going to have to be done today when you get home from school."

With a defeated sigh, she slings her bookbag to the floor and heads back to her room to attack the dreaded chore. But when she opens the door, everything changes. Her room is spotless and a tray of cookies sits on her dresser with a note that reads, "SURPRISE! Love, Mom."

Do you suppose that child thanked her mother? Do you think she knew she was loved? And do you think that she knew from that day forward that somewhere, someday down the line, her mother would surprise her again?

So it is with our Heavenly Father. He delights in surprising us. He waits patiently for just the right opportunity to connect with us and to show us His love. The more we think of Him in this context, the more we will see Him in our lives, and the more we will be aware of the many things He will do for us. Your faith must be stronger than your doubt; otherwise, you may miss a miracle.

The actual names of some of the people mentioned in this book have been changed in order to protect their privacy.

# *Celestial Colors*

Sometimes when God gives us a dream, we receive encouragement. Other times He gives us guidelines or warnings of impending danger. But I remember one dream that had a life-changing effect on me.

As my dream began, I found myself walking through a field of multi-colored flowers. But these flowers were like none ever seen on earth. The blues were like crystal clear Caribbean seas, but more blue, vibrant and almost translucent to the eye. The reds were brilliant bursts of scarlet with an almost liquid quality. The purples were deep and regal, hinting of the majestic hand that had placed them there. And the yellows were miniature suns radiating outward, dripping their golden droplets of color amid leaves and grass that glistened like an emerald sea.

For what seemed like an eternity, and at the same time like only a split second, I gazed in awe at this meadow on the edge of heaven. I turned and said, "God, I've never seen such vibrant colors like this on earth. How is it that they have come to be?"

God's reply struck at the very core of my being. As I awoke from my dream, I still heard His words speaking softly into the heart of my mind.

"It is because, My Child, they gave Me all the color that is within them."

Upon awakening fully, I knew that I wanted to be like those flowers, that I wanted to bloom with all the color that was within me and give all my being to God.

I knew that God Himself had put that color in the flowers and they, through obedience, were giving every drop back. Some earthly flowers complain, "I didn't get enough sun." Or earthly people complain, "I didn't get enough love." As a child, I was abandoned. Deep in my heart, I knew those thoughts could stop me from giving all that God had for me to give. I wasn't going to settle for Satan's seconds when I could have God's best. So right there in that moment I said, "Take all of me. Make me into whatever You choose. Help me Father in my disobedience, for I have been a rebellious child."

# Chapter
# 1

# *The Attic*
---

*N*ightmares sometimes begin as beautiful dreams. It was like that for me. When I was almost three years old, a day that began as a sun-filled adventure with my mother ended in utter darkness. When I've told this story in the past, people often ask me how I can possibly remember it because I was so young. But I believe that some life experiences are so indelibly inscribed on the memory that they are impossible to forget, regardless of your age.

When I got up that morning, my mother surprised me by saying we were going to spend the day together. She had been working a lot lately, and I hadn't seen her nearly as much as I would have liked. She knew I loved animals. So when she asked me if I would like to go see a horse that did tricks, she knew I would answer yes. As we rode along the country road, I could hardly sit still.

"Is that where the horse lives, Mommy?" I would ask at every farm we passed. "Are we there yet?"

"Just a little further," Mother would answer.

The houses became farther and farther apart, and the road first narrowed and then turned to a gravel road. I was beginning to think we were going to run out of road before we found that trick horse's home. Finally, the car swung into a winding driveway. A huge oak tree stood next to the farmhouse, and the car drew to a stop right under the shade of that tree. I was so excited that I skipped and jumped all the way from the car to the porch and impatiently shifted my weight from one foot to the other as Mother knocked on the door. The farmer who answered the door was a big man of indeterminate age who greeted my mother and me in a very matter-of-fact manner.

As we headed towards the barn, he sauntered slowly as if he had no particular place to be, and sauntering is not what a small child does best. But the farmer wanted to show us around the farm a bit on our way to the barn. Even though I was very impatient to see the horse, I do remember one of the things he pointed out to us as we walked. It was a chicken coop. Inside was one very large rooster. I started to move closer so that I could see him better, but the farmer stopped me.

"Don't **ever** go near that chicken coop," he said sternly. "There's a big red rooster in there. Do you see him? He's got metal spurs on his feet because he's a fighting cock. And I'm warning you now, he would flog you to death if you ever got in his pen. So you stay clear of that chicken coop. You hear me, girl?"

I remember standing at the fence that ran between the path we were taking and the chicken coop and thinking, *I know I could make friends with that rooster if I had a chance.* My mother reminded me that we came to see a horse; so I left the rooster and taking my mother's hand, continued on down the path.

At last! We were at the barn.

"Wait here," the farmer said as he disappeared into the barn. Mother and I stood by the corral fence. I watched the barn door intently and finally the farmer emerged, leading the most beautiful horse I had ever seen. He had a long silky tail; and when he tossed his head, his mane flew in the breeze. He looked like a merry-go-round horse come to life. I watched, fascinated, as the farmer began to show us some of the tricks the horse could do. First, he took a pail and he turned it over on the ground. With a wave of his hand and the command, "UP," the farmer got the horse to put his front hooves on the top of the overturned pail.

I watched in awe as he showed me how his horse could count by pawing the ground with his front hoof just the right number of times, and how he could answer yes and no questions correctly time after time. After the last trick, the farmer had the horse bow right in front of me. What a wonderful surprise my mother had planned for me. I was so happy that I turned around so that I could hug her neck and thank her. But I couldn't do that, because when I turned around, my mother was gone!

"Where is my mommy?" I asked the farmer.

"She's gone," he said flatly.

I began to cry. Now the trick horse wasn't important any more. I wanted my mother. I couldn't understand where she was or why she had left me. She hadn't told me she was leaving, and she hadn't told me I was going to stay. In the past when she had left me with a sitter or something, she would tell me she was coming back. She would kiss me good-bye and reassure me that she would return. But this time she didn't do any of that. This time, she just disappeared and left me alone on that farm.

I was inconsolable. I don't know how long I cried that night, but my crying must have irritated the farmer and his wife. When I couldn't stop crying, the farmer opened up a door in the ceiling over the kitchen. They threw my blanket on the attic floor and shoved me up in the attic. Then they closed the door.

All the light went out of the room, and I was surrounded by darkness. The darkness seemed to have a life of its own, and I could almost hear it breathe. Fear began to build up inside of me in a way I had never experienced before. I was abandoned, alone in the dark, and I was not yet three years old.

I curled my body into a tight ball, drawing my knees up to my chest and wrapped the blanket tightly around me. The planks that formed the floor under my feet were rough and uneven, and a sliver made its way into my bare foot. I stifled a cry of pain and tried to hold my breath so that no monsters would know I was there. I could hear all kinds of noises in the darkness as I just *knew* there must be dragons and bears and lions out there in the dark, just waiting for me to go to sleep. I dared not close my eyes, for I was sure that I could see their eyes glowing as the monsters waited for a chance to pounce on me. I held my body so still my muscles began to ache; but I could still feel my heart beating wildly inside my chest, and beads of cold sweat broke out on my forehead. *Mommy! Where are you? Why don't you rescue me?*

Finally, exhausted by fear and grief, I fell asleep.

Bang! The door slammed open and a bright light hit me in the eyes.

"Get down here, girl," the farmer's wife shouted impatiently from the kitchen below. "I've set the ladder for you, now come on. It's time to get up."

I scrambled to my feet and looked around. I tried to remember where I was. The room I was in was still dark, but that bright light didn't come from windows or a hallway. It came up through the floor. Then I remembered. I had just spent my first night in the attic.

As the days passed, I adjusted to my attic existence. I don't remember much about the farmhouse other than being able to look down from the attic into the kitchen. I could watch the family as they sat at the table and ate, but I don't ever remember eating a meal at that table myself. I was still very afraid at first, but somehow I began to be aware that there was something or someone with me, protecting me and making me feel less afraid. At that point in my life, no one had ever talked with me about guardian angels; but now that I'm an adult, I really think that's what it was.

There were three boys who sometimes came to this farm. I don't know where these boys came from; but when they came, I was allowed out of the attic to play outside. Their ages varied, but I think they were between six and twelve years old because they reminded me of stair steps, each one slightly shorter than the one before. I remember that their clothes were ragged and dirty and they had an overall disheveled appearance. But what I remember most was that they were very mean. They hurt me in many, many ways. No one watched us as we played outside. I think the boys were supposed to be watching out for me, but that was certainly not what they did. They seemed to think that keeping track of me meant devising as many ways as they could think of to hurt me.

Since they knew no adults would be checking on us, they were free to do as they pleased. They delighted in dragging me around by my hair like an old rag doll, and took great pleasure in hitting me with sticks and kicking me. They repeatedly molested me sexually and terrorized me each time they came to the farm. I knew in my heart that they wouldn't hesitate to kill me if I ever told anyone. I never understood why they did these things to me. Like most children who are abused, I tried everything I could think of to make them like me, but that just seemed to make them more determined to hurt and humiliate me. They just seemed to thoroughly enjoy torturing me, and I had already started a pattern of blaming myself.

19

What had I done wrong? Oh, how Satan loves to turn things around. I was the victim. I was the one repeatedly sexually assaulted. I was the smallest, the youngest, the most defenseless and yet somehow even then, I thought I was to blame. It should come as no surprise that a small child cannot tell an adult she has been raped. Many grown women let their attackers walk the streets to strike again because they somehow blame themselves for being attacked. Satan is a *liar*, and he was lying to me.

As an adult, I saw the story on TV about a child in Memphis, Tennessee, who was killed by other children. Everyone seemed to find it so unbelievable. *How could this happen?* everyone asked. But I understood how it could happen. I lived through the same type of evil, and the fact that it came from other children did not change the fact that it was Satan's work. Those boys at the farm were so vicious in their attacks, and so determined to get what they wanted from me, that I had to play dead to get them to leave me alone. Day after day, I endured their assaults, and day after day, no one came to rescue me. One day it all became just more than I could bear.

I had been at the farm for many months. By the time I was nearly five, I had been going to visit the rooster in his coop on an almost daily basis. I was determined to make friends with Big Red. I had been talking to him through the fence, and had worked hard at getting him to like me. However, I did remember what the farmer had said about the spurs on his feet, so I had never tried to go in his pen with him.

On one particular day, the boys had been so very cruel to me, using sticks and all manner of things to molest me. I finally decided that it would absolutely be better to die with that rooster flogging me to death than to endure another minute of what they were doing to me.

I struggled to free myself from them and when I finally got away, I ran as fast as I could toward the chicken coop. Without a moment's thought, I flung open the door and shut myself inside with the rooster. Exhausted, I just sat down in the dirt in the middle of the coop. My long dark hair was disheveled and dirty; and my clothes had been torn by the brutality of their most recent attack, but I continued to sit there waiting for the rooster to end it all for me.

The boys all ran to the fence and were peering at me through the chicken wire, just waiting to see what Big Red was going to do to me. At that point, I didn't care. The rooster came over and walked all the way around me. I waited for him to strike. Then something really surprising happened. Instead of pecking me and flogging me with the spurs on his feet, the rooster simply touched my arm with his head. It was just a gentle little rub; I looked up into his eyes, and I knew with a certainty that I had nothing to fear from him. I just started talking to him saying, "I know you are my friend and you won't hurt me."

The boys had been watching all this time, and they weren't getting the show they expected. They could plainly see that the rooster wasn't hurting me, and their disappointment was obvious. I guess they thought the farmer had been lying all this time about how mean the rooster was; because they decided if the rooster wasn't going to hurt me, it would be safe for them to come into the pen and get me. If Big Red wasn't going to do the job for them, they would get me out of there and finish it themselves.

They slung open the door to the chicken coop and headed for me. They didn't get very far. They were barely inside the doorway when Big Red turned around. He saw those boys and he changed. All the feathers on his neck stood straight up, and he curled his feet into claws. His metal spurs shone brightly in the sun and he began to run. He ran headlong towards the boys standing stunned in the doorway. They turned and ran in fear from Big Red, and they just managed to shut the door before he got to them.

I was amazed at what had just happened. That was the day I found a place of refuge in a most unlikely place with a most unlikely champion—a chicken coop belonging to a big red rooster.

I heard the farmer's wife calling us to supper; and now that I realized I had a safe haven and a protector, I became bolder. I looked the oldest boy squarely in the eye and said, "You know what? If you poke me and hit me and pull my hair anymore, I'm going to wait until you're not looking and I'm going to let Big Red out." Knowing I meant it, the boys backed off.

After the incident with Big Red, things got a lot better. The boys found other things to do and let me fend for myself. If they did decide to go back to groping or harassing me, I'd quickly head for the chicken coop and they would give up. Big Red had become my playmate, my confidant, and my protector. God certainly does work in some rather unusual ways to protect His children. He can even use a big red rooster.

# Chapter
## 2

# $\mathcal{L}$eaving the $\mathcal{F}$arm

$\mathcal{I}$ stayed at that farm with no word from my mother until I was almost six. Just as I finally began to accept that she was never coming back, another surprise came my way.

The day began like all the others. But after breakfast, the farmer's wife took me aside. She said that she was going to give me a bath and clean me up. My mother was coming, she told me, and if I was all clean and if I was a very good girl, my mother might take me home with her. Oh, how I scrubbed and polished. I slipped into my prettiest dress and tried ever so hard to stand still while the farmer's wife brushed my hair.

Not satisfied to sit on the porch swing and wait, I ran down the driveway and stood looking up the road so I would be sure not to miss my mother. I stood for what seemed like an eternity, and still she hadn't come. Now that going home was so tantalizingly close, I was giving myself a pep talk and trying to think of just what I would have to do to get my mother to take me with her.

I reasoned that mothers do not like children that are a bother. *That's probably why I'm here,* I thought. *She probably left me because I was in the way all the time and I bothered her. So the most important thing for me to let my mother see when she gets here, since she hasn't seen me in so many years, is that I've grown up. If*

23

*she can see I've grown up and can now take care of myself, then she will know that I will not be a problem.*

*I must be careful not to beg*, I reminded myself. I had learned that a whining, begging child really annoys adults. So I told myself that it was very important that I not beg her to take me with her. I had to make her want me without asking her. I had to be clean. I had to say things that were nice to talk about and show her that I could take care of myself. Oh, how I pondered my situation, and how carefully I formulated my plan. I was going to do everything just right, and my mother wouldn't be able to resist taking me with her.

Finally, a car came down the road towards the driveway, and slowed to a stop right next to me. A man I'd never seen before was driving, and my mother was sitting on the passenger's side. I had to stretch my head around to see past the man and actually get a good look at my mother. Without really looking at me, my mother introduced this man as my new daddy. My eyes went wide with surprise and I turned to look at him. I had never known my real daddy, so I thought that this was just wonderful news. Not only might my mother take me with her, but I would have a daddy to love me as well.

I carefully studied him, and I remember thinking that he had a very kind face with a sweet smile. He leaned out the car window and talked softly to me. He had a friendly tone, and he encouraged me to talk with him. I talked about the farm since that was basically all that I knew. I was very careful not to tell them about the mean boys who had hurt me. In fact, I was ever so cautious not to say anything that I thought would make me seem to be a problem. I asked a few questions about what they had been doing; but five year olds tend to run out of adult-type conversation pretty quickly, and soon there was a very uncomfortable silence.

Standing there waiting in that silence, it hit me. They weren't getting out of the car, and I wasn't being asked to get in. Now I was beginning to panic inside. The reality of the fact that they might not take me with them was just beginning to sink in. I felt tears building up, but I wouldn't let even one fall. I had told myself that I could not cry. I was certain that if I cried, they definitely wouldn't take me with them.

It took all the courage I had to lean in through the open car window so I could look across and actually see my mother and ask the question, "Mommy, are you going to take me with you?" Her response was an immediate, harsh "*No.*" So sudden and sharp was her reply that my new daddy turned and looked at her in disbelief. He reached over, put his hand on her arm, and told her it would be all right.

"We can take her now," he said. "It will be all right."

But my mother's answer was even more chilling the second time. "No," she said. "I'm telling you no. I'm not ready for her yet. She'll have to stay a while longer."

Crushed, I looked at my new daddy. My heart was breaking and I remember wondering if he could see the pain in my eyes. *Oh, please beg for me. You do the talking, Daddy. Convince her that you can take care of me.* I wanted to scream and beg, but I forced myself to be just so still and really quiet while he pleaded my case. He kept telling my mother that I wouldn't be any trouble. He assured her that they could make do until everything got situated.

"No," my mother said again. "I'm telling you, I can't do it, and that's final." Then she turned to him and demanded that they leave. Fear rushed over me, and I kept trying to think what I could have possibly done wrong. I looked up at my new father, blinking back tears. He looked back at me, making direct eye contact.

25

"Trust me," he said. "I will be back to get you soon. I promise."

Somehow I knew there was nothing more that I could do to keep them from leaving without me, and I backed away from the car. As I stepped back to the side of the road, they drove away.

I stood in the same place where I had stood just a few hours before with such anticipation. Now they were gone, and I could feel tears that had been welling up in my eyes threatening to overflow. I kept blinking and blinking as hard as I could to hold them back; but I finally couldn't, and the tears flowed unchecked down my face.

I had tried so hard to do everything right. I had been clean. I had been good. I had been polite. But they never even got out of the car. The joyful reunion and loving hugs that I dreamed of never happened. I tried to tell myself that they had stayed in the car because they didn't want to hurt me. If they had gotten out and let me hold them, I might not have been able to let go. The emptiness that I felt as they sped off was indescribable. But of one thing I was sure. My heart broke that day–for the second time, as I was left again by my mother.

After that day, I went over and over in my mind what had happened. My daddy's last words to me had been that they would come back for me soon, and that had given me something to hang on to. He had given me hope. Oh, how I wanted to trust him like he said; but sometimes at night as I lay on the attic floor, my faith in that hope would waver. *What if they don't come back soon?* I thought. *What if Mother convinces him that they don't need me? What if I said something wrong that day? What if I didn't look right, or what if I really am trouble, and what if...what if they **never** come back?*

But my father was a man I could trust, as I would later learn more fully. And true to his word, they did return. This time, I wasn't told they were coming, so I didn't have that anticipation and that long wait. They just showed up, said they were taking me with them, and loaded me into the car. I was sitting in the back seat practically holding my breath, afraid that they might change their minds. But they didn't. I could hardly believe it was really happening. We were getting farther and farther away from the farm, and I finally let my breath out with a big whoosh. It was really happening. My mommy and daddy were in the front seat, and I wasn't being left behind.

After we had driven a ways, my daddy turned into a driveway and pulled the car to a stop.

"We're at your aunt's house," Daddy said. "We have a few more things to do before we take you to our house, so we're going to let you stay overnight here."

I'm sure he saw my disappointment because he was very quick to reassure me. "We'll be back to take you home at noon tomorrow, Antoinette. I promise. We'll pick you up at twelve sharp."

My mommy and daddy went in with me and introduced me. Since they stayed to settle me in, hugged and kissed me when they left, and promised again to pick me up the next day, I wasn't so afraid to stay.

The next morning I ran to my aunt's side of the bed and woke her, announcing I was hungry. She reached down and pulled me into the bed.

"What would you like?" she asked, smiling.

"Pancakes!" I squealed. "And can I have a cup of coffee? I have never tasted coffee!"

"I will let you taste it, but you are too little yet to have coffee. You stay here with your uncle, and I will call you when it is ready," she said as she left the room to prepare breakfast.

I snuggled down inside the comforter, and rested my head on my aunt's pillow–and that is when it happened. My uncle's embrace was not the kind an uncle should give his niece. So one more time, my little body was abused, and one more time I could not tell anyone. But this time there was no chicken coop to run to, no Big Red to chase away the predator. I was again a victim, and I began to mentally shut down.

I could only poke at the pancakes my aunt had pre-pared, and I was listless and quiet for the rest of the morning. A little before noon, we headed for a local restaurant where Mother and Daddy were going to meet us. I sat quietly at the table, and kept my eyes riveted to the front door. There they were! I stood up from the chair and was going to run and meet them, but I could-n't. I tried but my legs would not move. I tried and tried to make my legs work, but I couldn't, and tears began rolling down my face.

Seeing my predicament, my new daddy came and scooped me up in his arms. Polio was rampant in the country at that time; and when everyone saw that my legs appeared to be paralyzed, this was, of course, their first concern. Daddy took me straight to the doctor. They ran all sorts of tests and were able to determine it was not polio. My inability to use my legs lasted for two days, then disappeared as swiftly and mysteriously as it had come.

I was too young at the time to understand that it had been a physical reaction to emotional trauma. I only knew that I could walk again and that made me happy. Later, I would discover the deeper emotional scars that did not heal when my legs did. Once again, not talking about what had happened only added to my previous wounds already buried deep inside.

I was forty years old when I could finally bring myself to tell my father about the molestation by the boys on the farm and the morning in my uncle's bed. All he could do was weep. I knew at that moment what it meant when Jesus wept. For until that day, I had never seen my father cry.

I knew it hurt him not to be able to save me so I said, "It's okay, Dad. Let's read one of my favorite scriptures that I've held on to all of these years. Matthew 18:6 where it says, 'But whoso shall offend one of these little ones which believe in Me, it were better for him that a millstone were hanged about his neck, and that he were drowned in the depths of the sea.' (KJV) It sounds to me as if God takes this matter very seriously; and therefore, so should we."

The challenge for a stepparent is this: Can that grown child say to them, as I have said to my dad, "You loved me with an unconditional love."? Love covers a multitude of sins. I have talked to a lot of children who are off-spring of divorce and remarriage. I have too often found that the stepparent did not love that child well, or sadly in some cases, did not love that child at all. I was always taught that the parent knows what is best for the child. So who failed? The child or the adult?

If these damaged children are to heal and be a productive part of society, who will help them to become whole? I believe God never puts one-on-one for one. He never connects one stepchild with one stepparent to do a work in only one of them. He desires to work in both. Oh, what a challenge for that parent. The Scriptures tell us in Luke 12:48, "For unto whomsoever much is given, of him shall be much required...." (KJV) A child is a gift from God...no matter where they came from.

# Chapter
## 3

# *My New Dad*

*I* was almost six years old when my dad adopted me, and that was when the fun began. My new dad had a motorcycle; he put me in front of him, and off we went for my very first ride down the street. Next, he took me to the store and let me pick out some toys, including a little airplane that would shoot up into the air when you wound it up. It was just the right toy for a child living on an air base. Suddenly, I felt so free and so safe. I felt so many wonderful things, and I could even feel my daddy's excitement to have me as his daughter.

I was an emotionally damaged child; and although I was only five, I had become cunning and vindictive. I had needed both to survive, and I clung to them dearly as old friends. But the Lord had other plans. He would teach me new ways to replace these ill-formed character flaws, and today would be my first lesson.

"Antoinette," Dad called. "Come here. I have something for you."

I would learn that my new dad loved to give me presents and surprise me, and today was the first of many gifts of the heart my dad would give.

"What is it?" I asked excitedly, trying to peek behind his back.

"It's a kite," he replied. "In fact, I have two—one for you and one for me. Come with me, and I'll teach you to fly it."

I raced with him to a big airfield near the abandoned military base housing where we lived. The air base was a great place for a child, with lots of other children to play with. But, today, it was especially wonderful because the airfield was the perfect place for kite flying.

My dad had brought many balls of string so we could let our kites soar as high as they pleased. Dad patiently showed me how to run with the kite and encourage it to leave the ground and fly up, up, up into the heavens. Soon our kites were mere pinpricks of color in the bright blue sky, and they seemed miles and miles away. Yet my dad had even more to teach me. He showed me how to send messages to the kite. He placed a piece of paper on the string, and I watched in wonder as it crawled up the string to my kite.

We were having a wonderful time as the kites swooped and looped and danced from cloud to cloud. I never wanted this day to end. It was all too soon when he called to me.

"It's time for you to go in and take your nap. Let Daddy get his kite down first, and then I'll help you with yours. See those high power lines? If you pull your kite in too fast, you'll pull it into those lines and you'll wreck it. Wait for me and I'll get your kite down safely."

My instant reaction to his telling me he would help me was one of anger and rebellion. I thought I was such a big girl. I wanted my dad to know that I could do lots of things, and I could *certainly* bring down my own kite. With an "I'll show him" attitude, I began to wind and wind, faster and faster, pulling my kite out of the sky towards the ground. I was trying to beat him so that I could get it down before he could get there to help me. Then he would see how smart I was.

Oh, he saw how smart I was, all right. Instead of the triumphant kite landing as I had anticipated, I managed to do just what he had warned me might happen. I pulled my beautiful new kite straight into the high power lines. It was wrecked beyond repair. I was crushed. There I was with my new dad, and I had failed. The feeling was horrible.

My dad took my hand and spoke comfortingly to me as we walked back to the house.

"It will be all right," he said, but I wouldn't be consoled. I knew from past experience that nothing he could say could ever make it all right. The pout that I had placed on my face when my kite wrecked was still firmly in place when we went in the house and when I climbed into bed for my nap. My dad carefully laid his kite on the bed beside me, kissed me on the forehead, and walked out of the room.

As soon as he was out of sight, I quickly slid out of my bed. I tiptoed into his nearby bathroom and picked up his straight razor. I carried the razor back to the bedroom and approached my dad's kite. With all the skill I possessed, I cut very tiny slits in the kite. I drew the razor along the colored areas so they wouldn't show; but they would be destructive, nonetheless. When I was finished, I put the straight razor back in its proper place in his bathroom and returned to my bed. Now that my revenge was accomplished, sleep came easily and was sound and sweet.

After waking up, I stretched luxuriously, like a satisfied cat. I was just completing my last stretch when my dad appeared in the doorway.

"Baby," he said. "Can Daddy talk to you a minute?"

Now that I knew his kite was destroyed just like mine, I decided I could afford to pretend to be his sweet little girl again, so I said, "Sure."

"You know," he began. "This is the first week that I've been a daddy, and I am going to have a lot of things to learn about how to be a good daddy. Today I believe I made a big mistake, and I want to ask you to forgive me. While you were sleeping, I realized that you really are a big girl, and you could have gotten your kite down if I had given you time. I'm sorry."

What was this? No one had ever told me they were sorry. No one had ever admitted to me that they had been wrong or made mistakes. Now I was listening intently, just waiting to hear what he might say next.

"Honey? Do you hear me? I'm sorry and I want you to forgive me, because I know I was wrong. Sweetheart, I know you must be sad because your kite is gone and I want to make everything up to you, so I've decided to give you *my* kite."

Wait a minute! This wasn't what I'd planned. A few minutes ago, the kite I destroyed with the straight razor was my daddy's, and I had wanted it to never fly again, but now...Now, it was suddenly not my daddy's kite–it was MINE! I'd destroyed my own kite!

My mind raced. How in the world was I going to get that kite out of the house without him seeing that it was damaged? I didn't want him to know I had been so hateful and mean and had tried to ruin his kite. After his sweet apology, how could I ever let him know what I had done? For the first time in my young life, I was learning that there are consequences for your actions. It was a bittersweet lesson that my daddy taught me that day.

I can't recall how I got the kite out of the house after that, or how I explained why it wouldn't fly. I was just glad that my daddy didn't find out how vindictive I had been that day...or so I thought. It was thirteen years later, when I was eighteen years old, that my dad told me the rest of the story.

"Antoinette, I watched you that day when you put the slits in the kite with my straight razor," he said. He didn't need to say anything more.

All those years I thought he didn't know, but he had. He could have come rushing into the room and stopped me. He could have scolded me. He could have punished me. But that is not what he did. As he watched me vent my anger on his kite, what he saw was the damage that had been done to my personality, and the ugly things that I had locked up inside. He saw my pain. He listened as the Lord showed him how to reach that broken child, and how to coax her out of those dark places in a most beautiful way. This is just one of many lessons that my daddy taught me, as his Heavenly Father had taught him.

# Chapter
## 4

# *Running Away From Mabelee*

---

*M*abelee was a very important person in my life, although it would take me years to understand just how important. She was only seventeen years old when she first came to work for my dad. She was not too tall and had an attractive figure. Her skin was like polished ebony, and she had a pretty face with beautiful teeth. She kept her hair short, sometimes with braids plaited tightly to her head. I remember her always being so clean and neat in her appearance. She had a sweet, patient nature with everyone. But I certainly didn't think she was very special the first day I met her.

At the time, I was finally back with my mother and my new dad, who had just adopted me. But like most families, my parents couldn't just stay at home and play with me. Mother and Daddy had to go to work. They needed a babysitter, and that babysitter was Mabelee.

I had never really had a babysitter before. Actually, now that I think about it, I had never really had a mother and daddy either. I'm sure I didn't realize it then, but this short time in my life was invaluable because it would be as close as I would ever come to having a whole family. I say a short time, because my mother left us again when I was ten, so we were together as a family for not quite five years.

Mabelee took her job very seriously. What she didn't know was that I didn't. The first second her back was turned, I was out the back door in a flash. It didn't occur to me at the time that there was anything wrong with this, since no one had ever come looking for me before.

Since we lived on an abandoned air base, the housing was one row of buildings after another and I was quickly and easily out of sight. To me, the air base was an adventure land, and I was as an adventure-loving a child as had ever been born. There were so many places to investigate. With my imagination running wild, I spent all day looking for adventure. I went from building to building, from group of children to group of children, and worked hard at my job of playing. I found kids to play with everywhere. At one house, I joined a crowd of children and got lunch, and then I stood in line for snacks at another house.

I saw Mabelee several times throughout the day; and each time, I scurried away and hid. I heard her calling my name over and over, but I never answered her. I was free and I was having fun. I was not about to give up my freedom and go home with Mabelee. Finally, I began to get quite tired and seeing that it was getting late in the afternoon anyway, I headed back home.

When I walked in the door, I found Mabelee on her knees. I came up behind her and as she turned around, I could see she had been crying.

"Lord, child. I cannot believe you are home. I have looked all over this base for you. I've looked all day and couldn't find you. You just don't know how you have worried me."

"Well, I'm home now," I said calmly, not really understanding what all the fuss was about, but also being wise enough not to tell Mabelee that I had seen and heard her.

"Yes, you're home now, but I didn't know what had happened to you. I was afraid to call your parents because I didn't know if someone had gotten you. Don't you understand, child? I was responsible for you! I needed to know where you were–to know you were safe! You just don't do this to people. You can't put somebody in this position!"

"I don't understand, Mabelee. I was fine. I was fine...and no one ever looked for me before."

"But I didn't know you were fine. I walked and walked and walked looking for you. You can't understand what that is like. I thought of many horrible things that could have happened to you. You can't do this any more!"

Fearing for my newly-found freedom, I pleaded with her.

"Mabelee, please don't say that to me. I need to go play with the children. I can't just sit in here all day."

"But you can't worry me like this either, child. Don't you understand?"

"Okay," I agreed. "But let's make a deal."

"What kind of deal?" Mabelee asked skeptically.

"We won't tell Mommy and Daddy what happened today. And from now on, I'll make sure I always tell you where I'm going. Then you will know where I am and you can even get a phone number so you can check on me. You'll be able to find me, I promise. I won't hide from you anymore if you will let me have some freedom."

After considering my proposition, Mabelee reluctantly agreed. "We'll try it tomorrow and we'll see how it works. Just remember, child, you can't ever do this to me again."

It was a simple agreement, but it was one that laid a solid foundation for a long-term relationship. I knew I had seen her many times that day, and that I had hidden just because I wasn't ready to go home. But when I did get home, I saw her tears. I did not fully understand the fear she felt, nor the responsibility she took so seriously–but what I did see was that my quest for freedom had caused Mabelee's pain.

But Mabelee saw beyond herself and focused on my need, putting it before her own. She put aside her own hurt and anger from this frightening and frustrating day, and decided to trust me on my terms. No adult had ever done that for me before, and I was determined not to let her down. From that day forward, I never did. A day that began with a rebellious child seeking satisfaction of her own need for freedom ended with my first experience with trust. Being trusted allows you freedom to trust someone else as well. And because of Mabelee's selflessness, a new kind of love began to sprout in my heart. Mabelee would become a mother figure to me as time passed, but today it was such a wonderful feeling just to be trusted.

# Chapter
# 5

# *Dicky's Story*

We had moved into town and into our first real house with my very own bedroom and yard. As I became more comfortable with my new home and family, I began to acquire quite a menagerie. I have always loved animals, and it never occurred to me that living within the city limits should limit the number of animals any one little girl should have. So with no restrictions in mind, I began my animal collection.

I realize now that I was very blessed no one complained; because the last time that I counted them, I had forty-seven pets. There were animals of all descriptions in my private zoo. I had dogs, cats, birds, fish, chickens, turtles, ducks, and rabbits. And then there was Matilda, my pet goat that I had brought back from my uncle's farm. Oh yes, I certainly wouldn't want to forget to mention the badly wounded mallard duck that I had nursed back to life. In a moment of childlike inspiration, I christened the mallard with the name Dicky, and we became inseparable.

I really had about three favorite animals that were with me all the time. There was a three-legged collie dog named Duke. Duke had the misfortune to have been shot in the leg, and the leg had to be amputated, but it didn't seem to slow him down much. He seemed to love

41

Matilda and Dicky almost as much as I did. It was a rare thing indeed to see any of the four of us without the other. In fact, when I had to go to the grocery store, Duke, Matilda, and Dicky went with me. Now that I look back on it, we must have been quite a sight.

When I got to the store, Matilda and Duke would wait patiently outside by the door, but not Dicky. Wherever I went, he went, especially when I went in the store. Dicky knew just where the seed sacks were, and he always headed straight for the spilled corn. He feasted on this treat from the minute we got there until I called him to go. We'd pick up Duke and Matilda at the door, and the let's-go-home parade was on. Animals can be such faithful friends, and Dicky was an especially good example.

My dad's business was just behind our home, and he walked to work every morning. I was still at the breakfast table one morning when he suddenly came back into the kitchen.

"We are going to have to rename Dicky," he said. "Maybe we can call him Dickerina since he—excuse me—*she,* just laid an egg."

"Really, he laid an egg? You're kidding!" I said as I shot out the door and ran to Dicky's pen. I picked up the surprised duck and danced with it in my arms.

"This is great!" I shouted. "I will eat it for breakfast. But Daddy, I still want to call him Dicky because he comes to his name."

Every morning after that I would run to the pen, and every morning I had an egg for my breakfast. But on the tenth day, what I found horrified me. There was another egg, but this one had a very transparent shell. You could see the yoke right through the shell. Wrapping the egg gently in a towel, I ran to my dad's store.

"Daddy, close the store! We have to take Dicky to the vet. She is very sick."

"What's wrong?" he asked, and I showed him the egg.

"Oh, I see," he said, inspecting the egg carefully. Then he turned to me. "Honey, we can't take a mallard to the vet. It won't help."

"Yes it will, Dad. I'll pay with my allowance. I know he can do something. Please. *Please!*"

I must have sounded truly pitiful because my father finally agreed. "Okay, but we have to wait until my relief gets here."

When we finally got to the vet, he listened patiently. After I told him my story, and my Dad confirmed that the duck had, indeed, been laying an egg every day, the vet turned to me with kindness in his eyes. He smiled as he assured me that Dicky would be just fine; and despite all my fears, my precious mallard duck was not dying.

"You see," he explained. "Ducks are not made like chickens, and they cannot lay an egg every day. Evidently your excitement over the egg, and your duck's love for you caused her to keep producing eggs until she ran out of shell-making material. She needs gravel to make more shell. She has gone to the limit to show you how much she loves you, child."

I've never forgotten Dicky's unconditional love, and her willingness to give her all for someone she loved. Animals can teach us so much, and I'm thankful to see that the medical field, especially, is utilizing animals more and more for therapeutic reasons. Just look through your Bible and see how God used ants, the ox, the lamb, the lion, the donkey, the eagle, and more to teach us great spiritual truths. A gentle dove is sent to represent the Holy Spirit, our Comforter, and He tells us

43

He cares about whether or not a tiny sparrow falls. There are many dynamic teachings that we are given through animals in the Bible; and if we look closely, we will see that God still uses animals to reach us in our daily lives.

God often uses birds and animals to show us great teachings, and that is why I love God's choice animals so much. Each animal is chosen to demonstrate a specific teaching, and each one is the perfect illustration as God sets it before us. The eagle is an excellent example of God's teaching on marriage. The female eagle tests her potential mate to the brink of death before she will marry him. He must go through a series of tests; and if he fails just one, she will not mate with him. The beautiful part is that all the tests have to do with her babies.

When a potential suitor presents himself, she picks up a stick about twelve inches long and flies ten thousand feet in the air with it in her beak. She begins flying a figure-eight pattern and he follows her. Suddenly, she drops the stick. As a gentleman, he flies down and catches it in mid-air. This "game" continues as she brings up larger and heavier branches, dropping them at ever lower and lower altitudes. The last stick weighs almost thirty pounds, which is about her own weight. But now she's only about 500 feet above the ground. If he can still catch it in mid-air, he has proven himself worthy.

The Scripture tells us in Deuteronomy 32:11 that we are to note how the eagle stirs up her nest, and in Verse 12 of that same chapter, God likens Himself to the eagle. So I believe we have something to learn here. "As an eagle stirreth up her nest, fluttereth over her young, spreadeth abroad her wings, taketh them, beareth them on her wings: So the Lord alone did lead him...." Deuteronomy 32:11, 12)

When the eaglets are old enough, the mother eagle throws her babies out one by one. Circling high above the nest in an ever-widening figure-eight pattern is the daddy eagle. Now the purpose of that pre-marital testing is clear. That last large heavy stick that fell so fast was practice for the real thing. Now one of his nearly grown babies is falling fast, and he must swoop under that baby and catch it on his back at the last minute before it hits the ground. He will then take it back to the nest for another try until it learns how to fly. But his timing has to be perfect, for if he catches the baby too soon, it will never fly.

We should do no less for our children. But often instead of testing a prospective marriage partner, a person just jumps into a relationship without thinking ahead. All too frequently, especially in remarriages, we develop a relationship that is just like the old one, still not recognizing that only the partner, not the problem, has changed. Especially when there are children involved, it is essential that some very important questions be asked and answered.

When marriage is considered, whether it be a first marriage or a remarriage, children should be part of the advance planning. Too often people marry with no thought of what kind of parent the other partner might make. In remarriages, you are dealing with children of divorce who have already experienced pain and rejection, sometimes at very early ages. How many parents, with the children in mind, truly test what kind of parent that prospective spouse will be?

My parents divorced when I was ten and my father didn't remarry until I was nearly twenty-two, so I really didn't have to deal with being a stepchild while I was growing up. After my mother left, Mabelee was free to serve as my mother figure without the difficulty of being a stepparent. But my brother grew up with a stepparent and my children had to deal with stepfathers. I see firsthand the damage that is done by having untested mates. If I had only let the lesson of the eagle override my own desires, the outcome might have been different.

If only one person can learn from this and avoid the temptation of marrying a person who would be an unsuitable parent, it will be a victory.

As for me, I can only pray that the damage done to my children will one day be healed. I thank God every day for the wonderful father I was blessed to have raise me. Even the Heavenly Father says we are adopted and we are encouraged to call Him Abba, Father. (Romans 8:15)

I have gone to the animal shelter and adopted two kittens, each with its own distinct personality. They, in turn, adopted me and have given back unconditional love. They sense when I'm sick or emotionally hurting and they lay beside me with a quietness that assures me they know. So I ask you, if animals can adopt you and love you and you aren't of their species, why then can't people just love people?

# Chapter
# 6

# *The Bus Ride*

There were many special times with Mabelee, but there were some that had a lasting impact that resonates within me to this very day. One of the first of these involves a time when Mabelee was preparing to go into town to do some shopping, and I did not want her to go without me. Although I was nearly six, I had never been to town so I pleaded with her to let me accompany her.

"Please let me go with you. Please, please, please!" I begged. "Daddy, make Mabelee let me go with her. I want to go into town, too."

"Baby girl, Mabelee takes care of you all the time," my dad answered. "Don't you think she deserves a little time off, even if it's just to go shopping by herself?"

"But I won't be any trouble. I promise I won't. Mabelee, I'll be good. Really I will. Pleeeeease take me with you?"

"Oh, child. Will I ever be able to say no to you?" laughed Mabelee, shaking her head. "Mr. Lewis, if it's all right with you, I don't mind if she goes with me."

My heart skipped a beat, and I jumped right in to put a little more pressure on my Dad. "Oh, Daddy, please say yes. Mabelee doesn't mind, and I'll be soooo good and...."

"Enough," Daddy interrupted. "All right. You can go. But you must be on your best behavior."

"I will. Don't worry," I told him and I went to my room to change my clothes.

"I will watch out for her, Mr. Lewis," I heard Mabelee tell Daddy, and I paused just a moment to listen because I didn't want my Daddy to change his mind. "I can assure you. I won't let that child out of my sight," she continued.

"I know she'll be safe with you, Mabelee, but I don't know if she's ready to see what the real world is like."

My dad knew me well. That day my innocence and childlike acceptance of things was to be challenged, and no one had really prepared me.

Now knowing it was truly settled and that I could go, I quickly changed my clothes. By the time I was ready, Mabelee was already at the door.

"Slow down, child," she gently chided me. "What are you trying to do? Get there ahead of me? Come now, let's have a look at you."

I had dressed in my Sunday best, and brushed my hair until it glowed in the morning sun that swept through the open front door. Mabelee adjusted my hair ribbons and sent me into the kitchen to say goodbye to my dad. I came skipping back excitedly and we both went out the door together for our adventure.

I'd never ever been to town before, much less ridden a bus, and as we walked to the bus stop, I barraged Mabelee with questions.

"What's it like to ride a bus, Mabelee? Is it fun? Do you think I'll like it?"

"Well, that sometimes depends on who you are, but you'll see. I think you'll like it okay."

She'd hardly finished speaking when we reached the bus stop, and a big bus lumbered to a stop just a few feet from us. I started excitedly towards the door, but Mabelee held me back and let some other people who were standing there get on first.

"We were here before they were," I remember complaining.

"Shush, child. Just get on the bus now."

I scrambled on the bus and plopped down in the front where we could look out the front window. Thinking I had managed to grab the best seat available, I called out to Mabelee, letting her know that I found us a dandy place. To my surprise, Mabelee walked right past me, with her eyes cast down and took a seat way in the back of the bus. Not understanding what was wrong with where I was sitting, I got up and went back to find out.

"I can't sit up front with you, sweetheart. Those seats are reserved for white folks. I have to sit in the back in the colored section."

I was stunned. I had never considered that the color of Mabelee's skin could make a difference about where she could sit on a bus. I thought about the situation for just a moment. If Mabelee couldn't sit in the front seat and look out that big front window, then neither would I. I scrambled up into her lap and announced, "Then I'm going to sit with you."

"Antoinette. You can sit up front if you want to. I don't mind. It's just that on buses there are seats for white folk and seats for black folk. No white folks sit in the black seats and no black folks sit in the white seats. Do you understand?"

No. I didn't understand, but I respected Mabelee enough not to make a big scene. I wouldn't ask her to move, but I intended to take the whole trip seated firmly in her lap.

It was a sweltering hot day and when we finally reached our stop, the first thing I wanted was a drink of water. I quickly spied a drinking fountain and headed straight for it.

"Help me up, Mabelee. Help me up."

Mabelee lifted me up so that I could reach the water fountain. The cool water tasted like heaven. When she put me down, I stepped back from the fountain so she could get a drink. She didn't move.

"Aren't you thirsty?" I asked.

"I can't," she said, pointing to a large sign above the fountain. "That sign says FOR WHITES ONLY."

I remember well the sick feeling I had in the pit of my stomach when she told me that. Mabelee was the closest thing to a mother I had and she had been hurt. You don't say bad things about anybody's mother, and you don't mistreat her when her child is around. God had a very special way of teaching me that day what prejudice really means. Only the heart of a child, innocent to the ways of the world, could really feel the emotion of those moments at the water fountain. But I have never forgotten those feelings.

As a grown woman, I now see the source of prejudice and it's called *HATE*, the opposite of *LOVE*. So, who is the father of hatred? Satan! Do you really believe your spirit or soul has a color? How about the heart? One Scripture I love speaks of how God looks on the heart: "...the Lord seeth not as man seeth; for man looketh on the outward appearance, but the Lord looketh on the heart." (I Samuel 16:7–KJV) I don't ever remember a Scripture where it says, "but God sees the COLOR."

# Chapter
# 7

# MGM Hollywood

*I*n addition to my animals, my childhood was much like a fairyland in many ways, and I was princess in residence. My father had previously worked in Hollywood for MGM; and when the studio purchased new equipment, they would auction off the old cameras and other equipment. It was at an MGM auction that he bought one of those sit-on-your-shoulder, wind-up kind of movie cameras that you see in documentaries about the early days of movie-making. My dad only had a tenth grade education, but he had vision, and was not one to let a good business opportunity pass by. Needless to say, I thought he was the most handsome, smartest man alive.

One of his business ventures involved the purchase of a very large corner building on the black Main Street in our town. At the time he bought the building, segregation was in full swing; there were no white people walking on that street, or no black people walking on the white people's Main Street. Segregation meant nothing to my dad. People were people, he taught me, and there were good ones and bad ones, no matter what color you were. With a philosophy of racial equality ahead of his time, he just went out and bought that building, and opened a dance hall. It was the star attraction on Saturday nights.

Saturday mornings, he would take me with him to prepare for the evening's opening. It was quite a play-land for a child. We would go in and clean the dance floor, and my dad would stock the beer box. I could drink all the soft drinks I could hold, eat potato chips, and even feast on my very favorite treat: pickled pigs' feet. Then came Saturday afternoon.

There was a very special ritual that took place every Saturday on that Main Street. The ladies would come to town dressed in their very finest: their fanciest dresses and hats. Their heels would click as they strutted up and down the street, just as if they were on a catwalk at a Paris fashion show. That's when my daddy would get out that MGM camera and begin filming. Even with black and white film, you could see the shiny sequins, and almost feel the lushness of the velvets and satins that the women wore to the dance hall. With feathered hats and high-heeled shoes, they were ready to party.

Dad let me go with him a couple of times. And to this day, I don't think I've ever seen anything quite like it since; to me, it was just fascinating. It was an entirely different culture, but it also felt like it was part of my heritage, as well. I had never been taught prejudice and just accepted all the life experiences as opportunities to learn. After filming in the afternoon, it would be time to swing open the doors to the dance hall. It was always packed.

My dad always ran the films he had taken on Saturday afternoons on the following Saturday evenings. The movies he showed on a large screen of the local women decked out in all their finery became as much a part of Saturday night as the dance hall itself. I only got to go there a couple of times at night, and I had to stay upstairs in the office. But I got to peek out and see all the people dancing and enjoying themselves. It was exciting, to say the least. I don't know how anybody was able to move, much less dance, because it was so crowded in there.

Between Mabelee and my dad, it never occurred to me to feel out of place. I actually felt very much at home there. I loved that Saturday ritual, and I'm afraid it may now be somewhat of a lost custom.

Mabelee never went to the dance hall, so far as I recall. In fact, I don't think I ever saw her dressed in anything but a crisp, freshly-laundered white blouse and a slim, sensible skirt; but she was still beautiful to me. At the same time all this was going on, my mother began getting worse. She was an alcoholic, and her drinking was reaching its peak. As much as Mabelee wanted to be with me, Mother was requiring more and more of her attention. As a result, Mabelee had her hands full, and I was spending more of my time alone. With Mabelee otherwise occupied and Mother unable to help even herself, the pain of rejection began settling into me again. I know now that Mabelee was trying to protect me from seeing my mother's sickness, but still it felt like she had just left me. That old rejection spirit kept rearing its head.

Mabelee tried, but she could not shield me from everything. In fact, the day came when I was face to face with the worst of my mother's problems, and it was a day when I was all alone. I was about eight years old and had just come home from school. Mabelee was not at home, and I began to search for Mother. When I finally found my mother, she was lying on the bathroom floor with both wrists slit. Blood was everywhere, and to this day I have no words to describe the terror I felt.

I began screaming at the top of my lungs just as Mabelee came running in the back door after a trip to the store. As always, Mabelee took charge, taking me out of the room and calling the ambulance and Dad. My mother was taken to the hospital, where her wounds were tended to; I stayed at home with Mabelee, wondering if Mother would be all right. Ultimately, Mother was admitted to a sanatorium for treatment of tuberculosis, and my dad arranged to have her depression and alcoholism treated as well.

As soon as Mother was well enough to leave the sanatorium from a medical standpoint, the doctors tried to keep her so that they could help her overcome her alcohol addiction and deal with her depression. Mother quickly realized what they were trying to do, but decided she didn't want this kind of help. Every time my dad went to see her, she begged him to take her home. Eventually her persistent pleading and promises to change got to be more than my daddy could take, so he arranged for her to come home. With her alcoholism and depression still untreated, she came home to be cared for again by young Mabelee.

I was desperately lonely and longed for the times when Mabelee and I had chatted together and she had taught me to cook in the kitchen, but she was needed elsewhere now. But God had plans to care for me, as well. It wasn't long after Mother's return home that my dad's grandmother moved in with us. It is so like God to send another comforter. This time, He sent a ninety-year-old little old lady.

Today we have generation gaps, and many of our young people miss out on the treasures that older family members have to hand down to them. I was fortunate. My great-grandmother became a big help to Mabelee, but she spent the majority of her time being my constant companion, teacher, and playmate. She moved into my bedroom; and having her sleep with me helped me with the night fears and bad dreams that continued to plague me.

She had long silver hair, which she wore neatly pinned into a bun on the back of her head. When she let it down, it came down almost to her waist. Oh, how I loved to brush that beautiful hair, making sure it got at least a hundred brush strokes a night so it would be sure to shine. While I brushed her hair, Grandmother told me stories of the Civil War. Afterward, she would bring out treasures that she kept in her large dresser, among which was a beautiful walking cane with a silver head on it. The silver head was engraved "Jefferson Davis to L. A. Taylor, 1878." L. A. Taylor was Grandmother's husband. She told me of the wonderful parties and the fancy clothes that they wore, and how a lady of her day was expected to act.

I often wished that I had been born during that time as I heard these stories. The life she had known as a young girl before the Civil War seemed so serene and so beautiful, nothing like the world I knew. Grandmother spent many hours teaching me the etiquette of her day, and I feel truly blessed to have been her pupil. We have lost some precious traditions and could learn much about being a true lady from those women of the 1800s.

As things began to get worse with my mother, Grandmother shielded me more and more by diverting my attention. My dad would be gone most nights, looking through different bars, trying to find my mother. While he was gone, Grandmother would read me stories and tickle my back until I would fall asleep.

I had formed an early trust relationship with Mabelee, but now she was tending to Mother. Deep in my heart, I found I still could not trust people to be there for me. Trust was a big stumbling block for me, and God knew it. It was a stumbling block that even hampered my relationship with Him. But I finally found out that God is not like people. He is omnipotent. He is trustworthy, and He could be counted on to always be there for me whether I recognized it or not. I had finally let go and had begun trusting Grandmother, when she passed away in her sleep.

The morning that she died, I went across the street to my girlfriend Martha's house. Martha and I played together, and I think it was my way of seeking the familiar in the face of the absolute void created by my grandmother's death. Martha and I lay in the tall grass in the alley between the rear of her house and the front of mine. We watched the ambulance come and take Grandmother away, and Martha cried with me as we watched the ambulance roll out of sight.

Finally, I stood up and told Martha I was going back home. When I arrived, it was Mabelee who was immediately there for me again. It was she who helped with the grieving. I never had any problems with Grandmother's dying in my bedroom because she had been such a Godly woman. She had not been afraid of dying, and had talked with me about the heaven she expected to enter when she left this world. Her confidence in her final destination left me without fear from her death.

Once again I turned to Mabelee. I had thought she was just too busy for me with Mother when Grandmother had moved in. But in fact, she had deliberately stepped back just so that I could bond and learn good things from my grandmother. When I look back now, I can see that her love for me was big enough to share, and she knew that I would learn things from Grandmother that she could not teach me.

After Grandmother's death, Mabelee quickly let me know how much she had missed our time together. She began once again to let me stand beside her and learn to "soul cook," as she called it. By the time I was ten, I was really getting quite good at cooking all Mabelee's recipes, but most of all, I loved our time together.

I didn't venture out much in our neighborhood with other children, as my mother and her extramarital affairs were the talk of the town. When I did go out, I would ride my bike to what was referred to as "the other side of the tracks" or the poor side of town. In the seg-regated South, it was an area where the poor whites lived, but I was more at home with the children from this neighborhood than any of the other children in town. Their homes were filled with love and acceptance, and their lives seemed to me to be far more normal than mine. There I was accepted for who I was, not who my family was, or where I lived.

I loved to help with the chores these children did around their homes, and I felt like I was part of a large family. I remember when the chores were done, we would often get a special treat–a saltine cracker heated in the oven with mayonnaise on it. It might not sound too tasty to you, but I've had elegant desserts that couldn't compare with those crackers, because they were baked and given out of a heart full of love.

# Chapter
# 8

# *The Scrapbook*

*M*abelee often took me with her to visit her family. And while I loved my visits to Mabelee's family's home, there were still a lot of empty spaces in my own family history. There were voids that I felt compelled to fill. That's one of the reasons I went to see my Aunt Margaret.

Aunt Margaret was my mother's sister. Many of the stories that I did know about from my childhood I had heard from her. I remember sitting with her one day, looking at one of her old scrapbooks.

"What's that, Aunt Margaret?" I asked, pointing to a wrinkled old gum wrapper.

"Oh, that," she laughed. "That is a reminder of just the cutest story about you." She smoothed the gum wrapper with her index finger and began.

"When your mother and I were preparing to go to the grocery store, we always made a list. Then we'd take the list to the store and pick up the groceries, using the list. Evidently, you had been observing this ritual very closely; but apparently, you never noticed the money that changed hands for the groceries we brought home. In any event, this particular day we went to the store as usual. Apparently, you had found a Juicy Fruit® gum wrapper somewhere and had scribbled your 'list' on the back of it.

"While your mother and I were selecting our purchases, you went up to the grocer and handed him the gum wrapper. 'Candy!' you announced. The grocer just rolled with laughter. Your mother and I rushed over just as he was handing you your candy. I've saved that chewing gum wrapper list all these years as a reminder of what a smart little girl you were."

"How old was I when I did that, Aunt Margaret?"

"Well now, let me think. You couldn't have been very old because it was not too long after you were so badly burned. So, you would have been somewhere around two, I think."

"Tell me how I got burned, Aunt Margaret. I know I have a scar, but I can't remember what happened."

"Your father had already left. He didn't even stick around to see you born. He didn't want the responsibility of a family. Anyway, your mother and I didn't make much money. We couldn't afford a regular apartment at that time. We were waitresses in a restaurant, and that just didn't bring in enough money to meet all our expenses. We had a friend, though, who had a grocery store, and behind the store was a small building where they stored the coal that was used to heat the store. It was just a wooden shack, really. One part contained the coal bin where the coal company dumped the coal. Most places were heated with coal back then, you know.

"The other part of the building was just one room with a dirt floor. We had electricity, so we could cook on a hot plate; but we didn't have a refrigerator. We kept our perishables in the grocery store's refrigerator. But it was so close, it wasn't really inconvenient. It had one really important thing going for it, though. It was free! Free was what we needed.

"Did I ever tell you what we did with you when we were working? We couldn't afford a baby sitter, so we took you to work. You were such a little thing when you were a baby that we cleaned out a deep drawer in the restaurant where they were keeping silverware. We made a bed for you in that drawer, and that's where you stayed while we worked."

"Aunt Margaret, what was it like in the coal shed? What did we have in there?"

"Basically, darlin', we didn't have anything. We did have an iron bed and your playpen. There was an old wooden table with the hot plate on it. In fact, that's how you got burned. You can't tell it from the scar you've got left there, but you were burned very badly."

"How did it happen?"

"Well, your mother and I were making starch for our uniforms. Back then we made a home-cooked starch from flour and water. You cooked it to a boil, and it made a thick substance that you would use on your clothes as a starch. That was what was cooking in the pot on the hot plate the day you got burned. You were in your playpen, but it had been moved too close to the hot plate. You reached up and hit the pot's handle, and the hot starch poured all over your face and body. Your little body began to convulse and your mother screamed, scooped you out of your playpen, and ran for the cab stand in front of the grocery store.

"I sprinted out behind her and we grabbed a cab to the hospital. It was winter, and there was snow and ice on the ground, which delayed the cab driver somewhat. Your mother stuck her index finger in your mouth to hold your tongue because she was afraid that you would swallow your tongue during the convulsions. By the time we reached the hospital, you had gnawed her finger to the bone. In fact, that's where the scar on her finger came from.

61

"When we arrived at the hospital, we ran in. Your mother had you in her arms, and she ran up to the nurse's station and screamed, 'Save my baby! Save my baby!' Very calmly the nurse told her that she would have to have a fifty dollar deposit. Money was something neither your mother nor I had, and your mother was in a panic by this time. She took off running down the hall looking for someone, anyone, who would help you. There was a man dressed in scrubs coming out of the operating room and your mother, assuming he was a doctor, thrust you into his arms and said, 'Save my baby. I'll be back with the money.'

"There was a pawn shop not far from the hospital, and your mother went there. She took off her winter coat, which was one of the few really nice things she owned, and pawned it for the fifty dollars she needed for you. As soon as we got back to the hospital, she took the money straight to the nurse who had demanded it in the first place. 'Here's your fifty dollars,' she said.

"But the nurse refused the money, and snapped at your mother. 'You don't have to pay,' she said. 'You knew exactly what you were doing when you brought that baby in here. You knew who that man was when you left your baby with him. You knew that his father owns this hospital. That baby's going to be taken care of, and it's going to cost you nothing. Like you didn't know that already.' In a huff, she turned her back on your mother and me, and we just looked at each other in disbelief."

"You mean they took care of me for free!"

"They certainly did. You had plastic surgery and everything. That's why you don't have any scars on your face."

"That's amazing! There is something else I do remember, Aunt Margaret. It happened after Mother and I had moved to an apartment, and before she took me to that farm. I remember that apartment in detail to this

62

day. In fact, I described it to Dad not too long ago, and he was astonished that I could remember it so clearly. But a traumatic event took place there, so that's probably why it's indelibly imprinted in my memory.

"I remember looking out through the bars of my crib and seeing my mother across the room. There was a man in the apartment, and he was hitting my mother in the face, over and over again. I yelled 'No! No! No!' and I was crying very loudly. My fingers were wrapped tightly around the crib bars, and I'm sure I was shaking the crib with everything I had in me.

"'Shut that brat up, or else,' the man shouted at my mother. 'You shut her up now or I'll take care of her, too!'

"Mother rushed over to my crib, and pried my hands from the bars. 'Hush, little one. Shhhh! Be still now,' she said as she gently laid me on my back. 'No more crying. Be a good girl and go to sleep. Shhhh.'

"I've sometimes wondered, Aunt Margaret, if that had anything to do with why my mother took me to the farm. I think I was probably just in the way."

"I'm not sure that her decision had anything to do with any one thing; but I do believe, though, that your getting burned was at least a part of the reason your mother gave you away."

"Was I too ugly after the burns? Did she begin to hate me then?"

"Oh no, child. You misunderstand. She gave you away because she loved you."

"Loved me? Then why would she give me away?"

"Let me try and explain. Your mother was very young when you were born, really still a child herself. Her husband had abandoned her, and you. And she didn't really know how to take care of a baby. But she loved you and was determined to do her best. Just a few weeks before you were burned, your mother had fallen asleep with you lying on her stomach. In her sleep, she rolled over and threw you off the high iron bed onto the dirt floor. She was sure she'd killed you. From then on, she became more and more afraid that you were going to be hurt or killed in her care. Then, you got burned. For your mother, it became a catalyst...a sign that you were in danger in her care.

"There is often more to a story than what it appears to be on the surface. Your mother's actions may have been an extreme reaction to her circumstances. But whatever you think about your mother, whatever mistakes she made, know this. Your mother loved you. She released you out of love to protect you, and it was probably one of the hardest things she ever did."

# Chapter 9

# Rags To Riches
# To Rags

*I* identify very strongly with the Biblical Joseph. I can relate to his life and I believe I know how he must have felt. Joseph's brothers had thrown him into a pit and sold him into slavery, so he was abandoned by his own family. Then he was unjustly confined in prison by Potiphar for a crime he did not commit. I was an innocent child, abandoned and imprisoned like Joseph. The attic was my pit and the farm was my prison.

But then, when Joseph was at his lowest point, Pharaoh selected him to oversee the wealth of his kingdom. Now Joseph had a life of luxury. So it has been for me, as well. I had lived nearly three years in the attic, and then my new dad made my world my own personal fairyland. I had my own skating rink. It had a pump organ that I loved to play music on. I also had my own ice cream parlor with an ice cream machine so I could invite my friends for free ice cream and skating. In high school, I had a new Cadillac to drive, and I was able to wear beautiful clothes.

But all these *things* did not bring me acceptance among my peers. I longed to be popular like the other girls, but all the wealth in the land could not bring out a personality that I had never developed. I had learned to be a loner in my formative years in the attic; and now, in high school, I was still a loner most of the time. So as wonderful as these luxuries were, they could never fill the empty places in my heart, especially that large void that longed for family. What I desired was a storybook kind of family, and that was hardly the case with my own family.

When I was fifteen, my mother left town with another woman's husband. So our little community was just buzzing with gossip about my family. It was gossip that lasted throughout my junior high and high school years, and it was gossip that I did not want to hear any longer. Although my adopted father was a great father to me, there was no way that he alone could give me the kind of family my heart desired.

I knew my now-divorced father would probably want to marry the woman he had been dating soon, and I was very uncomfortable with the thought of living with both of them. The bottom line was that these rumors were killing me, and I wanted to get away from them. So I left to live in Memphis, where I attended both business college and modeling school. Then, at nineteen, I surprised my Father by announcing that I would be getting married.

The young man I had decided to marry was a virtual stranger; but to my star-filled eyes, he was the love of my life. I had met him over Christmas break. His sister was my best friend at the time, and I met Danny through her. Danny and I actually dated for about two weeks before he left to go back home to North Carolina. But over the next year-and-a-half, our relationship flourished through the letters we wrote each other. Now I was going to marry him. In doing so, my world would once again change drastically.

Danny was far from rich, and I would have to give up all the luxuries I had grown accustomed to in my father's house. I would be going back from riches to rags. But I thought I was "in love" and I convinced myself that it didn't matter. After all, love makes everything perfect, doesn't it? In any event, I was ready to grab for the stars and run away with my sweet Danny. I would soon learn that running away was not always the best answer.

It never occurred to me that after our wedding, we would be moving into the house with his parents in Arizona. My new husband did not know about what I came to refer to as "the Night." In fact, I would be married almost a month before I could bring myself to confide in my husband about that night.

It happened not long after Danny returned to North Carolina. His father, Harvey, called me. He told me that he had gotten a letter from Danny asking for the family's blessing because he wanted to marry me. Harvey asked if I would like to see the letter and read it myself. Of course, I wanted to read it. I could hardly wait to see it. Danny's father offered to bring it over to my house. But when I mentioned that my Dad was not home, and would not approve of my letting any men come in when he was not at home, Harvey was ready with an alternative suggestion. "No problem," he said. He offered to just pull in the driveway and honk the horn. Then we could drive down Main Street or towards the air base while I read Danny's letter. I agreed.

Danny's parents lived all the way across town, yet he was there in less than five minutes. I was so excited about reading the letter that it did not even register that there had not been enough time for him to make the drive from his house to mine. I opened the car's passenger door and slid into the front seat. Not wanting to seem like an anxious teenager, I didn't ask about the letter immediately. I began to chatter away about other things, and for a few minutes he just listened. Then he

67

began to speak. As he spoke, his words slurred and I was suddenly aware of the strong smell of alcohol. Harvey, it would appear, was quite drunk.

While I mentally chastised myself for not being more observant before getting into a car with a man who had been drinking, I was slow to realize where we were going. Finally, I noticed that we were headed towards a desolate road out near the air base; and with that realization, I began to be afraid and my heart began to pound.

Trying to remain calm, I said, "Well, I think it's time to see that letter, don't you?"

"There's no letter," he said. "I'm going to show you a good time, though." My mind raced as Harvey clearly detailed everything he intended to do, and I looked around, trying to find an escape route. He swung the car sharply to the right and pulled the car to a stop in a secluded area. Before I could react, he reached behind me and locked the door. He pulled me roughly down onto the seat. I realized that screaming would do no good, as the spot was too isolated for anyone to be near enough to hear me.

I must try to talk to him, I reasoned. I tried to remind him about Danny and how he would feel. Harvey paid no attention to my arguments, and continued to push himself on me, ripping my blouse off and sending the buttons flying. Realizing that I couldn't talk him out of it, I began to fight back. In order to hold me down in the seat, he bit me on my chest. I began to bleed, but I was fighting for my life. I kicked him in the crotch as he was trying to get his pants down, but he still fumbled his way onto me. Fortunately for me, he was too drunk to do much of anything but run his hands all over my body and slobber alcohol-laced kisses on my skin.

One last time, I tried to reason with him. "My dad will be home soon, and you'd better let me get back before he does. If he sees me like this, with blood all over me and my clothes all ripped off, he will kill you. I left him a note telling him I would be with you." I realize now that I took quite a chance by saying that, but in this instance, it worked. Harvey straightened up and without looking at me or saying a word, he started the car, and drove me home. When he pulled in my driveway, he grabbed my arm and threatened me.

"Remember this," he said menacingly. "If you tell your father, this will hit the papers and your reputation will be ruined. Nobody will ever date you again without thinking that you're 'easy.' And they will all want one thing. Besides that," he slurred on, "if there's a fight between your dad and me over this, he could be killed. Then where would you be?"

I jerked my arm out of his grasp and ran in the house, locking the door behind me. Daddy had not gotten home yet, so I quickly washed the blood off my chest and put on a high-necked blouse. I hurried to the kitchen and found a brown paper bag. I threw my ripped and blood-stained clothes into it and stuffed the bag as deeply into the outdoor trash can as I could. Then, before Daddy could get home, I went to bed.

As a young child, I had learned to put myself in a deep sleep to escape bad thoughts and frightening things that had happened to me. Once more I used this technique. The one thing I could not do was tell my dad. I didn't want him to be disappointed in me. I don't think I realized at that time that I was the real victim.

The next morning was Saturday. I was supposed to go see Danny's sister, Brenda; but I couldn't face anyone, and I had no intention of going anywhere. Finally, I called her to say I was sick. Her mother answered the phone. It was evident, even over the phone, that she was crying.

"We are leaving," she said. "Harvey is like a wild man. I don't know what has gotten into him."

I knew only too well what Harvey's problem was. The family had been planning to leave on Monday for their new home in Phoenix, Arizona, but now Harvey was insisting that they leave immediately. Brenda and I said our good-byes over the phone and they were gone. I don't have the words to explain the relief I felt when I knew Harvey had left town.

It was months before I could tell anyone about "the Night," but I finally did confide in my Aunt Margaret. She said she wasn't surprised, but that I should stop blaming myself. "Harvey is a crude man," she said, and she told me he had even tried the same thing on her. After I pleaded with her to keep my secret, she reluctantly promised not to tell my dad.

Despite what his father had done, I was sure I still loved Danny. Now I wanted more than ever to run away with the man I thought I loved. I wanted to escape and I thought that Danny was the answer. I could see us now, sitting on the porch of our vine-covered cottage, loving each other forever. There was one thing that Danny's father had said that horrible night that I just couldn't get out of my mind.

"Now you will never marry Danny," he had told me.

I couldn't understand why any father would want to hurt his son so much. But his telling me I would never marry Danny presented me with a challenge, and I didn't back away from a challenge. If Harvey thought his threats could stop my wedding, I was determined to prove him wrong. I would not be intimidated, and Danny and I were soon married.

It would be twenty years before I learned why Harvey hated Danny so much, and was willing to do anything to hurt him. Danny's mother had gotten pregnant with him while Harvey was overseas in the military. Danny was not his son, and Harvey would torture Danny all of his life because of it.

I sometimes wonder if I had known these things while we were married if it might have made a difference. But Danny and I never talked about such things. We both had traumatic and dysfunctional childhoods. Neither of us had the parental role models that we needed. Danny's father never taught him how to be a father or a husband, and my mother never taught me how to be a wife and mother. Because we failed to communicate about these deep emotional scars, Danny never knew of the abuse in my life, and I never knew his childhood had been spent sleeping on the floor while his sisters had beds to sleep in.

If I could have seen ahead or known how ill-prepared I was on my wedding day for the important decision I was making, I might have listened more carefully to my dad before I married Danny. Dad and I were in the back room at the church, preparing to walk down the aisle. He turned to me and tried to hand me a wad of one hundred dollar bills and the keys to his new Cadillac.

"Take this," he said. "Go wherever you want. Just let me know you are safe. I will walk out there and tell them you are gone. This is a little boy you are marrying, Antoinette, and he will never take care of you."

"Please, Dad," I pleaded. "Please be happy for me. I am nervous enough as it is. I love Danny."

"I am begging you," he continued. "One more time, I'm begging you. Don't marry this boy. He is damaged, damaged more than you know."

I knew my dad was an excellent judge of character, and he had always been able to see things I never saw. But I was headstrong and determined. I should have trusted his advice, but I was too intent on escaping. The money and the keys went back in my Dad's pocket. Shaking his head in frustration, he took my hand, kissed me lightly on the cheek, and walked me down the aisle to wed Danny.

Oh, how I wish Daddy had been wrong. But the first week we were married, Danny bashed my head into a closet door, breaking the wooden slats. Instinctively, my hands went up to my head, and when I brought them down and looked at them, my hands were full of blood. Danny ran out of the house when he saw the blood on my hands. I began screaming, and continued to scream, but no one came to help me. I ran to his parents' kitchen with my bloody hands extended. I couldn't understand why someone didn't help me. After all, we were living in his parents' home at the time, and surely they must have heard. Yet no one could give me a valid reason why they did not help me.

Danny eventually came back to the house. And since I had nowhere else to go, I stayed with him. My father had remarried, and had married the woman whose husband had already left her and married my mother. I just couldn't go back to that. We were only living with his parents until our apartment was ready, but it became a house of horrors. Danny's father was always quick to try and catch me alone in a room. With no one around, he would grab at me and pull my blouse up, making some coarse comment like, "I just wanted to see if you had grown any."

Danny was so afraid of his father that I couldn't count on him to come to my rescue. By now I had told Danny the whole story about the night his father had attacked me, and made him aware that his father continued to make passes at me. But Danny refused to confront his father, even though I begged him to "please make your father stop." I still didn't know that Harvey was not Danny's real father, so I found it hard to understand the fear that man had instilled in him. He had taken a innocent, helpless little boy and made him a slave. I thank God that we only had to stay with his parents for a few weeks, and then we were able to get away from that monster.

My new apartment just became another prison, however, for Danny had learned from his father how to be abusive. I worked as a maid at night, cleaning apartments at the complex where Danny was the groundskeeper. During the day I worked at a hardware company, handling the invoices. Still the fights with Danny continued. Danny was very controlling, and I was not allowed to go out except to the grocery store and work.

Eventually, we moved to North Carolina and I became pregnant. Danny even beat me when I had our baby in my arms, and that became a turning point for me. For the first time in our five years of marriage, with virtually all my self-esteem having been beaten out of me, a spirit rose up in me when I realized that my child was also in danger. Like a lioness protecting her cubs, I took my son, Joseph, and I walked out. Now I had someone who needed my protection besides myself and I drew upon a new strength.

But I'm sorry to say that I took a coward's way out instead of God's way. I had an affair as an escape route and used it as a safety net for me and my child. I had not yet learned that God has escape routes we can use. Just as Sarah took things into her own hands and caused a big mess by giving Hagar to Abraham, I caused years of hatred, turmoil, and damage to all my sons that would be given me.

# Chapter
## 10

# Steven's Story

I walked out of the courtroom after getting my divorce from Danny and into the Justice of the Peace's office the same day. I was through with Danny and went immediately into a new marriage with the man with whom I had had an affair. And with that, I became Mrs. Brad Forrester.

Brad and I immediately left for Jacksonville, Florida, where Brad was stationed as a pilot in the Navy. Life seemed so different. There were no more beatings, no more tortures and punishments. I could now actually go shopping and have friends. My first husband's need to control me had made this type of freedom a rare occasion in my first marriage. I finally felt free once again!

Brad and I had moved to Maryland right after we were married, and I soon discovered I was pregnant. Much to my delight, Brad had previously adopted Joseph, my son from my first marriage. Joseph's real father had quit paying child support for his son the day I got married to Brad. He never saw it as "his child that he was abandoning." He only saw withholding money and not seeing his son as a way to hurt me for leaving him.

Since we were only about three-and-a-half hours from our hometown, I insisted on having the same doctor that delivered my first child. I did see the doctors on base for routine prenatal check ups, but somehow I felt more comfortable with Dr. Gardner's actually delivering my baby.

I was in my eighth month and Brad had just come home from deployment in the Mediterranean. We were sitting at the kitchen table our first morning together since his return. Something had been bothering me for some time. Now that Brad was home, I knew it had to be addressed.

"What would you do if this baby is born deformed or retarded?" I asked bluntly.

"Don't talk like that." His shock and surprise were clearly evident. "All mothers worry that something will be wrong with their babies, but everything will be fine. Just don't talk like that."

"I asked you this question for a reason, Brad. Please answer me."

"I wouldn't do anything but love it," he answered decisively. "But let's not talk about this now."

"I have to, Brad. There is something wrong with this child."

"How do you know that? Have the doctors said something?"

"No. It's just that this baby will not play with me. When I was expecting Joseph, I would get in a tub full of nice extra warm water. I would fill the washcloth with water and let it drip on my stomach. Then Joseph would lift up his elbow or a knee or something, and it would poke out on my stomach. I would take my fingers and tickle very lightly, and then I would move the spot an inch and start tickling there. He would move whatever he was poking and again a little bubble would show up on my stomach in the new spot. I would tickle him again and then move again, and he would stay right with me. This baby tries to communicate that way, but its movements are like slow motion. Instead of poking and jumping from spot to spot, it flops over inside me. There are no fast movements from this baby."

"I think it's your imagination," Brad said, obviously relieved, believing that my method of determining this problem was far from scientific.

"Well, since you've never carried a baby inside you," I began somewhat defensively, "I wouldn't expect you to know that I communicated with my unborn child through touch and that this baby is trying, but it can't do it."

"Please, Toni. Put this out of your mind. It isn't good to think like this."

"Now that I've told you, I'll be fine. At least now you will know my thoughts."

Since I had endured three days of extended labor with Joseph, plans were made to induce labor for this child on April nineteenth. In the delivery room, Dr. Gardner told me that the baby was crowning, meaning that he could see the top of his head.

"What is it?" I asked, ever so anxious to know if I had a son or a daughter.

"Wrong end," Dr. Gardner joked.

At two o'clock in the afternoon on April nineteenth, my second son, Steven, was born. But unlike my first child, this baby did not cry. Dr. Gardner stood up and carried him across the room and laid him in a small bassinet. He continued to lean over the baby, and I realized that I still had not heard even one cry.

"Dr. Gardner," I called out anxiously. "He isn't crying. What's wrong?"

Returning to me, Dr. Gardner tried to reassure me. "Not all babies cry," he said.

"Well, I *insist* that my baby cry."

Dr. Gardner got up again, went over to the baby, and spanked my baby to get him to cry, but what I heard sounded more like a tiny puppy's yelp than a healthy baby's cry. I knew the difference between what Joseph had sounded like and the faint, short "waah" that this baby had made.

I was about to ask more questions when the nurse gave me a shot that put me to sleep. When I woke up in Recovery, five other mothers who had delivered about the same time I had were being wheeled from the Recovery Room. Dr. Gardner appeared in the door for the first of three times.

"Have they had a chance to get you cleaned up yet?" he asked from the doorway.

"No," I replied. "And I haven't seen my baby, either."

"We had to put him in an incubator for a while," he told me, and as quickly as he had appeared, he disappeared. It was as if he didn't want to hear any more questions. He came by a second time and again asked if I'd been cleaned up. When I asked again about my son, he told me that the baby had been "blue" and said he would need to remain in the incubator for a few more hours. I wanted to ask him more questions but before I could say another thing, he disappeared again.

The third time he entered the room, he finally walked over and stood beside me. Taking my hand in his, he said, "This is the worst part of my job, but I have to tell you something. There are three pediatricians looking at your baby, and it appears he has some of the characteristics of a Down Syndrome baby."

"I've never heard that word," I told him. From the look on his face, I could tell this was not good news, but I had to know so I asked directly. "What does it mean?"

"You may have heard about babies like this when you were in school, but in your textbooks they may have called them Mongoloid babies," he answered.

He was right. Mongoloid was a term I had heard, and at that moment I realized what he had been trying to tell me. I remember that it felt like the room and my bed were getting bigger and I was getting smaller and smaller, sinking down, down, down into this huge mattress. Dr. Gardner was still talking, but I couldn't hear his words. Only the one word kept ringing in my ears. *Mongoloid.* I felt myself drawing away from reality and going to a place I had never been, a place that was far, far away from the real world. Then I began to cry. As Dr. Gardner saw what was happening, he rang for a nurse. Just as I felt as if my heart would pound out of my chest, the nurse administered another shot and I sank gratefully into unconsciousness.

When I woke up this time, my sister-in-law was sitting beside my bed and she was crying.

"I've been to see him and I don't see anything different in him. I think the doctors are wrong."

"Karen, I know that you love me and want to encourage me, but I don't think Dr. Gardner would have told me this if he hadn't been sure. I know he said that the baby's missing some Down Syndrome characteristics, but I just don't know which ones. Dr. Gardner says he has enough of the characteristics to be sure of his diagnosis. What I do know is that I'm being punished for my adulterous affair with his father."

"That can't be, honey. That just can't be. I didn't get punished for my affair."

"I'm not saying God punished me, Karen. I am saying that my sin opened the door for the accuser of the brethren. Satan could have chosen to hurt me in many ways...in my finances, my own health, or even my children. I believe that Satan chose my child as the path he would take to try to destroy me. It's like the door David opened when he desired Bathsheba, Karen. That's a 'sin doorway.' It allows Satan to come in. Bathsheba was the wife of another man, and David had him killed so he could marry her. They lost their first-born son to death. Our son hasn't died, but I feel that he will never be totally with us, either."

By now, Brad had finally reached my room. He had gone looking for Dr. Gardner. He was furious that he had not been with me when the doctor told me about the baby's condition, and had let the doctor know in no uncertain terms that he should have been at my side when I heard the news.

When we learned about Steven's Down Syndrome, I thought I would somehow miss that special mother-child connection that I had anticipated. Boy, was I mistaken. Steven taught me more about being real than anyone I've ever met has been able to do before or since. Through this little child's sweet, loving nature and his ability to forgive, I began to see the world in a whole new way.

The joys a mother experiences with a normal baby are a given. The milestones appear when you expect them. You know they will take that first step, say those first words within a certain normal time span. As a mother of a retarded child, I found that I was always surprised when those milestones happened for Steven, and there was a very special joy in each and every one.

Steven was three years old, and still had not said even one word. He could crawl and get around fairly well, and had even mastered walking. He just wouldn't talk. He would make a noise if he wanted something. He would point at the refrigerator and say, "Ahhhh, Ahhh," but no real words. When I would open the refrigerator, I would point to different items, using the process of elimination to determine just what he wanted. I would watch him closely, for he would get a very excited look on his face if I pointed to the right thing. He wasn't talking, but we were communicating.

There was one thing that made finding the right treat in the refrigerator pretty easy. Most of the time, Steven wanted bologna. One particular day, I was running behind. I had gotten a sitter just so I could run to the store. Sometimes I took all of the children with me, but Brad and I now had a third child, Bryan. So with three boys now, I needed a sitter when I had to hurry. When I returned, I carried all the groceries in the house and let the sitter go home. I checked on the boys and found Steven in the den watching cartoons. My other two were in the backyard playing. I was almost finished putting the groceries away when I realized I didn't remember putting up the bologna. By now, I was buying the giant economy pack, so it certainly wouldn't have been hard to spot. *I know I bought it,* I told myself. *Could I have already put it up and in my haste, not even realized it?* I opened the refrigerator and scanned the shelves. No bologna.

Suddenly it hit me that everything seemed a little too quiet. I'd worry about the whereabouts of the bologna later. Right now I figured I'd better go into the den and check on Steven. He was probably still watching cartoons, but I needed to be sure. I stood in the doorway to the den, amazed at what I saw. Without thinking, I yelled, "Steven, what have you done?"

Startled, but smiling, he looked up at me. On his right, was a stack of the red rings that go around the outside of pieces of bologna. On his left side was a "mile-high" stack of bologna that had been de-ringed. He had separated them, preparing to eat. Having gotten his attention by yelling, Steven looked at me standing in the doorway. He took his right index finger, and pointed at the huge stack of bologna he had assembled.

"Bologna," said my child in a clear voice, as if he had been talking forever.

There was no way I could be angry with him now. I was so excited. He had said a word. Steven had said his first

81

word! I ran over to him, picked him up in my arms, and swung him around in a circle.

"Yes! Yes, Steven!" I kept saying. "You're right. It's bologna, bologna, bologna...."

There were many surprises this child gave me, and each one is a beautiful memory that I carry in my mother's heart.

Things did not go well in this marriage either, and eventually I found myself once again divorced. Now I was going to court for custody since I had only taken Joseph in the beginning. After I secured a job and a place to live, I thought it would be easy to go back for Bryan and then Steven, but I had to have special sitters and a lot of things in place. I never counted on Brad remarrying right away and a custody battle to ensue. This time Brad called my ex-husband Danny to speak against me. Both men wanted payback, but I never expected them to try and extract it from my son instead of from me. If I had, I would never have let Joseph go to the courtroom with me that day.

Before the court date, Brad had offered my son something he knew Joseph really wanted. A bright, shiny, new motorcycle could belong to him. All he had to do was leave me and agree to live with Brad. Joseph refused. He wanted to live with me. So on this day, Brad stood up in the courtroom, in front of everyone present, disowned Joseph, and said that he would have the adoption legally set aside. Joseph and I were both stunned. But it was not over. In that same courtroom on that same day, Joseph's natural father, Danny, made it clear that he didn't want Joseph, either.

Joseph was sitting in that courtroom, and had just heard both the men he had called Daddy say they didn't want him. I knew what rejection could do to a person, and Joseph was rejected twice in one day. My heart ached for my son. Oh, how I wished I had not taken him to the courthouse. My child was only eleven years old.

In my opinion, that judge was acting very strangely. First, he had refused to let any of my seven witnesses give any testimony at all. He didn't let Brad have anyone speak for him either. I do know that Brad had the boys, Steven and Bryan, hidden, so that Bryan could not be called to testify and say that he wanted to live with me. My attorney had formerly been a judge, so I was sure that he knew how the system worked. But he had apologized to me about what he described as "the deals they are making behind closed doors." He said that since he was not an attorney in the county where the case was heard, he did not have the leverage that Brad's attorney had. I guess I really shot myself in the foot, because after almost ten years of marriage, I had signed over the house and everything. I only wanted my children, but the only child to go home with me that day was Joseph.

Now I had no husband, no home, and a job that required me to travel throughout five states. I guess I didn't look too good to that judge with respect to my home situation, but I had one thing that neither of my ex-husbands had. I had a mother's heart full of love, and I wanted my children at home with me. I wonder if that judge knew that a little nine-year-old boy was going to be shipped off to a camp for delinquent boys as soon as Brad got custody. I've often wondered if that was part of "the deal" that my attorney was talking about. If that judge didn't know, he should have; and if he did know, he should be ashamed. In any event, the day after the court hearing, my son, Bryan, was gone.

When we got home, Joseph broke down, crying.

"Doesn't anyone want to be my daddy?" he sobbed.

"Please forgive me for being so stupid as to take you in that courtroom, Joseph. I did not know that your real father would be there. I had no way of knowing Brad and Danny would do this. I can never erase what I have done this day, Joseph, or the pain you suffered in that courthouse, but

God Almighty can and will. You were hurt for things that *I* did, not you. I know you are too young to understand now, but it will be my constant prayer that someday you will truly understand how Satan uses the minds of people."

There was really nothing I could say, but I did know that I was looking at a full-blown generational curse in action, and it was hitting both my sons at the same time. Now I was reaping what I had sown, and my heart hurt in a new way with an indescribable hole there now. When you hurt your own heart, you can reach in and pull out the fiery dart. You can even insert emotional ice into the wound to stop the bleeding. Then you come to a place where you realize that your Maker can put His warm hand on your heart, melt that ice, and heal your wound if you will but let Him. Then the healing can begin.

But you must remember that His ways are higher than your ways. So how He does it is His deal, and you just have to let go and let God. If it had been just my own heart that was hurt that day, it would have been different. But this damage was done to my two sons' hearts, and I could not see where the dart was, nor where the ice might be. It would be years before these mistakes would play their way out in my children's lives. All I have been able to do is pray and wait for God to show His path, inch by inch.

Joseph had come home with me and I comforted him as best I could. Brad had managed to keep custody of Steven and Bryan, the two sons we had together. So that day, it was just Joseph and me against the world.

Sometimes I dream of Steven. In my dream, I play with him and we have a wonderful time together. When I wake up, I feel like it really happened, and it helps fill the hole in my heart. I do have consolation in this, however. I know that Steven and I will eventually be in Heaven together, where I will be able to see him and hold him and play with him–and where Steven will be made whole and perfect in body, mind, and spirit by the King Himself.

# Chapter
# 11

# *The Gift*

$\mathscr{I}$ had just been transferred in my job from Raleigh to Burlington, and everything seemed to be in a state of upheaval. I hardly knew anyone in the area; and when an acquaintance asked me if I'd like to go to a party to try and meet some new people, I jumped at the chance. We partied for a while at a local restaurant, and then everyone seemed to be headed elsewhere.

"Come on," said one of my new friends. "We're going over to Jody's place and everybody's invited." I was sitting on the couch in the living room when Jody made her entrance.

"I heard this voice from out in the kitchen," she said, "and I just wanted to see who it was. My, but you're a little thing for such a big voice, aren't you?"

As I looked up at her from my seat on her couch, I was struck by how much she looked like Barbra Streisand to me. *So this is Jody*, I thought. She was such a free-spirited woman and I admired her confidence in herself, especially with men. This was something I wanted to learn. I would later find out that within herself, Jody was not sure she was really as free as she pretended to be, but her judgment of men was right on.

Jody's apartment was much like her life. It was filled with an eclectic blend of antiques and trendy things. There were bright colors everywhere and hardly a place to sit down. Strays poured in and out the door like it was a hotel. Some were cats and dogs, to be sure. Even a small, injured baby squirrel had been nursed back to health here. But many of the strays were strangers who needed help. Jody never asked anything of them, and few actually gave back to Jody even a portion of what she provided for them.

In fact, by the time I met her, Jody had already been lied to over and over, had her generosity abused, and had been stolen from and conned. Still, she continued to give and give and give. It seemed to her that to not give would be like asking her to stop breathing. She needed to help others to live. Jody had a gift of mercy. Unfortunately, mercy is also a gift easily abused, especially by those who perceive a giver such as Jody to be an easy mark for their treachery.

After I arrived that day from Raleigh, Jody insisted that staying at her apartment just made sense. After all, everyone was welcome here. What was one more? I was concerned about being an imposition, but I was grateful for her offer. Not only did I enjoy her company, but it would allow me a couple of days to look for an apartment, as well. By now, I was exhausted and somewhat beaten down from the most recent changes in my life, so I gratefully accepted the purple afghan Jody handed me and fell asleep almost as soon as I lay down on the sofa.

By eight o'clock the next morning, I could sleep no more. My first goal was to get a bath and feel refreshed from yesterday's trip. I was pleased to find everything I needed in Jody's small, but well-stocked, bath. Locking the door, I ran the warm bath water and lit several of the many candles Jody had surrounding the tub. After a relaxing bath, I towel-dried my hair and body, and began to dress for the day. I was just finishing the final touches to my hair and make-up when I was startled by a loud banging on the door.

"Hey, you in there! What do you think this is, your private hotel or something? Somebody else might need to get in, too!"

I flushed with embarrassment and quickly opened the door.

"Wow! Where did you come from? You look like a model or something. Hey, Jody, where'd you dig up this fashion plate?"

Jody quickly hurried to my side. "Don't let him bother you, Toni. Apparently no one ever taught him any manners."

"Who is he?" I asked.

"Haven't a clue," Jody replied. "He needed a place to stay and there was a sleeping bag in the hall, so I let him crash here."

"Aren't you afraid to let strangers in?"

"I let you in, didn't I? And just where would you be, Princess, if I hadn't?"

"Well, of course I appreciate it. It's just that I would never...."

"Never is a long time, Toni. Today is about all any of us can handle. Come on, let's find something for breakfast."

Over the next few days, I began to take the first steps towards a friendship that would be unlike any other. Jody was one person who took me at face value, but she did tease me constantly about always being "Miss Perfect."

"Don't you ever relax?" she would ask. "We're only going out to the grocery store. Do you really need all that makeup and the high heels just to get milk and eggs?"

"A lady must always look her best," I would reply.

"Yeah," Jody said, "but who wants to dress like that all the time? You can be a lady even when you wear jeans."

I didn't really see it then, but my "being a lady" was part of my armor against the pain and hurt of rejection. The result of my beauty regimen had a dual purpose. It drew people to me, yet it also served to keep them at a distance. I really was insecure and I think I needed the praise and admiration I could draw with my flawless makeup and pretty clothes. I had been a model, and I knew how to take advantage of my face and figure; but at the same time, I felt I could not afford to let anyone close enough to see who I really was. I saw myself as anything *but* beautiful.

My methods had always worked before to protect me from any honest relationships, but Jody was different. She saw right through me and she still stayed by me. Eventually, she broke down my barriers and I let her in. I had never had a true friend before, but then I was blessed with Jody. She didn't know how to be any other kind of friend but real. Over time, I began to open up to her. There was nothing judgmental in her; and for the first time in my life, I had found a friend with whom I felt safe.

There was one night in particular that I remember. It was a quiet night early in the fall when I finally shared with Jody the stories from my childhood, including the time I spent in the attic.

As I finished my story, Jody let out a long breath which she had been holding for some time. "Wow!"

"I truly believe that God was watching over me even before I knew who He was," I told her.

"Okay," Jody said. "I believe He works in mysterious ways to protect His children, but I never heard you talk about God before. Why now?"

"Well," I answered. "I didn't know what you'd think and I didn't want to lose my only friend."

"You wouldn't lose my friendship because you believe in God," Jody replied. "I was brought up in a Christian household, too. My parents were in church every time the doors opened."

Relieved that she understood, I was just beginning to relax again after the emotional drain of sharing these difficult times with my friend when the phone rang. Jody jumped up and grabbed it on the second ring.

"It's for you," she said, holding the receiver out to me.

"Who is it?" I asked, wondering who would even think to look for me here. Jody shrugged her shoulders, indicating that she really didn't know.

"Hello?" I said tentatively. Instantly I recognized my younger brother's voice.

"Sis," he said. "I hate to be the one to call and tell you this, but our mother is dead."

Totally shaken by his words, I finally managed to ask, "How? She's so young. How could this happen?"

"It was cancer, the fastest growing kind. We didn't know, Antoinette."

I hung up the phone with my brother's words still resounding in my ears. I couldn't believe it. She couldn't be dead. She just couldn't. I began to cry.

Jody was immediately at my side, her eyes asking the question that I answered before she could speak.

"My mother's dead, Jody. I can't talk to her. I can't hold her. I can't tell her that I know why she did the things she did. She will never know that I forgive her." My voice broke as I was overcome with emotion.

"Dead? Toni, I am so sorry."

For a while, Jody just held me in silence. Finally, as my sobbing subsided, I told her what was on my heart.

"I now know that she loved me in the only way she knew how. I know the truth, but now I have no mother. I really don't know how I feel inside."

"Come on," Jody insisted. "We're going out."

"I don't want to go anywhere," I protested, stunned that she would even suggest it right now.

"I'm not giving you a choice this time," Jody responded.

I had learned long ago that arguing with Jody when her mind was already made up was useless, so I reluctantly picked up my coat and followed Jody out to her car.

"Where are we going?" I finally asked after we had driven for several minutes in silence.

"We're going home," Jody said simply.

"Home?"

"That's right, Toni. We're going home."

She turned her little car into a narrow driveway on the left and came around to my side and opened the door.

"We're here."

"Where is 'here'?" I asked.

"This is my mother's house. I'm bringing you home to meet her."

"Don't you think this is kind of a bad time to introduce me to your mother? I'm not at my best to meet people, that's for sure."

"Trust me. It's the perfect time," Jody responded.

Jody rang the bell for a split second before opening the door and announcing in a loud voice, "It's me. Jody."

"Jody! Thank you, Lord. My Jody's here."

This, I surmised, must be Jody's mother. She was a plump little woman with silver hair that was curly like Jody's, but much shorter. She wore one of those fancy cover-all aprons so favored by 1950s TV homemakers. She brushed flour from her hands, and explained that she had just finished baking an apple pie and that we were just in time. She never asked us why we had dropped in so late in the evening, or why her daughter had brought an uninvited guest. She just bustled us into her kitchen and set a slice of warm pie in front of each of us.

I watched as Jody and her mother talked. They seemed to pick up in the middle of an ongoing conversation. There was a relaxed and comfortable feeling between them, and I couldn't help being a bit jealous, especially tonight. Why would Jody bring me here on the very night I found out my own mother was dead? If it had been anyone but Jody, I might have felt it a cruel thing to do, but I knew Jody well enough to know that she would never do anything to deliberately hurt anyone. There must be another reason. But if there were, I couldn't seem to see it. Despite the longing in my own heart, I did find that I enjoyed the visit quite a bit. Jody and her mother drew me into their conversation, and I was surprised to find I was actually sad when Jody told her mother we had to go.

"There's just one thing I need to do first," Jody said. Grabbing my hand, she placed it firmly into her own mother's hand.

"From this night forward, Toni, my mother is *YOUR* mother. She will love you and treasure you as only a mother can, and I will forever be your sister."

This was such a special gift from Jody, and I knew deep in my heart that once again my Heavenly Father was giving me another family.

Jody's parents became immediate parents for me. Papa and Mama accepted Joseph as if he was their own grandchild. They loved to babysit. Papa would lend me money when I was in trouble, and Mama taught me to make a special chocolate syrup that she would serve over hot biscuits. I will never forget the Christmas that Mama presented me with her "daughter's quilt." Each of her own daughters had been given a homemade quilt, and now it was my turn. The whole family knew she had been making one for me as well, but I was totally unprepared for such a "gift of the heart." When I unwrapped the quilt, I was overwhelmed. It was tangible evidence that God had again made me truly part of a family.

I was there when Papa passed away, and a few years later when Mama died. In fact, Jody and I traded off nights sleeping on a cot besides Papa's bed. I would go and check on him during my lunch hour. But the lunch hour I spent there after Hospice had come in and set up his hospital bed is the one I remember most vividly.

When I went into the room they had set up for Papa, I was dismayed at what I saw. All the window shades were drawn and everyone was standing around looking solemn and sad. Death had taken over that room before its time, and everyone seemed to have given in to it. *No way*, I thought. *Not yet. Not while I'm here.*

"Stay right there," I said to everyone, and I left as quickly as I had come.

My first stop was a store that sold posters. I bought several large ones, one with a beautiful sunset, another with glorious snow-capped mountains, and still another with a lake lit with sunlight. I picked up some potpourri and fresh flowers and went back to Mama and Papa's house. I went straight back to Papa's room and immediately opened all the window shades. I put up all the bright posters around the room, started the potpourri simmering, and placed the multi-colored flowers in a vase where Papa could seem them. As the light and the sweet fragrances began to fill the room, I could feel Death retreating, knowing he could not overwhelm us yet.

Turning to the very surprised family members, I said, "Now this is the way we are going to handle this. We all know that Papa is going to heaven soon, but he's not going today and he's not gone from us yet. Heaven is a glorious place of light and life, and we are going to make every second he has left on this earth with us as wonderful and happy as we can. Today is not a day of sorrow. It is a day to enjoy life."

When I finished speaking, I realized that everyone had been watching the transformation process in the room and they were weeping. But they were weeping tears of joy! We just never thought of doing it this way, they told me.

Papa was really mentally sharp right up to the day he died. Just three days before he died, he gave me a very special gift. I was standing beside his bed and we were looking at each other, just chatting. All of a sudden Papa's eyes widened in surprise. He was looking over my shoulder at something behind me. I automatically turned to see just what he was looking at. I saw nothing, but it was obvious he saw something.

"Do you see the light, Papa?"

"Yes, I do," he said. "And it's talking to me. It's telling me that I'm not ready. What does that mean?"

"Well I can't say for certain, Papa, but it sounds as if you probably still have something left to do. You have been such a strong support figure in this family, and such a godly man with your children and grandchildren. It could be something as simple as a conversation that you still need to have with your grandchildren. I can't tell you what it is, Papa, but ask the Lord. I'm sure He will tell you what it is, for He says in His Word, "My children have not because they ask not." (James 4:2 KJV)

Two days later when I got to the house for my shift, Papa was so excited.

"I know what it is!" he said.

"Wonderful, Papa! Tell me about it."

"It's my poem book that I'm leaving for all my children. The last poem is finished but I hadn't given it a title."

"Have you now, Papa?"

"Yes. The title is *The Last Page*."

Just a few short hours later, Papa died peacefully in his sleep. His last work on earth had been accomplished.

# Chapter
## 12

# *My Brother, My Brother*

*I* was ten years old when my brother was born. He was very sick and I was not allowed to go in the nursery to see him for many weeks. He had a heart defect and many internal problems, which were caused by Mother's drinking. Taking care of babies was very difficult for her, and shortly after my brother began to stabilize physically, she left the family.

I now understand that Mother had not had anyone to teach her how to be a parent. Her mother had died when she was born, and her father was a professional gambler. He would go off on the road for weeks on end and leave my mother and her sister, my Aunt Margaret, in the care of their two older brothers. Eventually, the children were found eating out of garbage cans in an alley, and the rest of my mother's young life was spent in an orphanage. My aunt told me stories of beatings they got each month just because they were having their period. She once told me that since Mother was so small, Aunt Margaret would throw herself over my mother to shield some of the blows.

They were finally released from the orphanage when Mother was sixteen and my aunt was eighteen. They later found out the woman in charge was not sane. With only this unstable woman as a role model all those years, Mother could not learn to love. When you have had no mother to love you, and when you had no love or attention given to you, how do you learn?

After our mother left, Harold's early life was as normal as it could be for a child who spent his formative years without a mother. He was very spoiled by our dad, and rightly so. Dad tried to make up to both of us for not having a normal home life and for our mother's absence. Mabelee had been a Godsend for me but she could not be there to help with Harold. Mabelee was dead. She had been attacked in an alley by a man who cut her throat and left her to die. This was another great and traumatic loss for me, and I sometimes wonder how she might have helped my brother if she had lived. We had different housekeepers with Harold, but none had a love to compare with the kind of love I had received from Mabelee.

Dad worked late most nights, and I was the one who stayed with my brother. I wasn't one of the popular girls in school, so my social life was not really hampered by staying home and taking care of him. If I did have a school function to attend, Dad saw to it that I could go. As soon as I graduated, I left for business college and modeling school. Harold was in elementary school when Dad remarried two years after I left home.

I am sharing these things not as an excuse for my mother. There are too many "excuses" out there in today's world as it is, and there is not enough self-analysis of our own actions that may hurt others. I just want people to know my brother, and to understand that he and I have forgiven our mother.

Eventually, my brother grew up and married. He has one child who has spina bifida, and he has proved to be a wonderful father. He is steadfast in his love and provision for his child, and I am proud of the man he has become.

At the time the following happened, my brother was on his third marriage and so was I. Knowing that we had some part in the failure of two previous marriages each, we weren't feeling very good about ourselves at this time. It did seem that with every mistake my brother and I made, we became closer and closer. Even when I was in North Carolina and he was in Arkansas, I knew when he was hurting. I could feel it deep down inside.

Lately, he had been on my mind a lot more than usual, and I had an undeniable sense that he needed my prayers now more than ever. He had not shared anything out of the ordinary with me; but somehow, I knew he was in trouble. Then came the dream.

It was in a dream that I was shown what was wrong. My brother's wife was having an affair with his best friend, and that best friend was also the pastor of their church. My brother had taken his days off to help paint the church. Side by side with this man, my brother had helped him prepare a garden. Harold loved this pastor like a brother, and he had faith in his friendship and his integrity. Now the dream showed me clearly how my brother was being betrayed. *How much more could he take*? I wondered. His ex-wife had cheated on him and it had ended that marriage. Now Agnes was doing the same thing.

I was very calm as I dialed his phone number the next morning. I knew that my brother would be at work and his wife would be the one to answer.

"Agnes," I said. "Are you on the kitchen phone?"

"Yes," she replied.

"Do you know which way is east?" I asked, my voice still remaining calm.

"I think so," she said.

"Well, turn in that direction and watch for a cloud of dust because I am going out to my car now to leave for Arkansas. On Sunday morning, I will walk up the aisle of your church and will go straight up to the pulpit. I will stand in front of your friends and neighbors, and expose to the congregation the adulterous affair you and your married preacher are having. So get ready!"

By the time I got to Arkansas on Sunday, that pastor had packed up his wife and kids and had moved away. I didn't need to make my announcement. He was no longer in town. He had resigned.

The problem with this pastor's solution is that to the best of my knowledge, he never repented before his congregation. He certainly never asked my brother for forgiveness. In fact, I understand he is preaching in another church now. But his actions, and those of my brother's wife, Agnes, turned my brother away from his church and began him on a journey of disillusionment with God.

There are so many people today, just like my brother, who are being wounded within the church, and some blame God. It seems that Satan's tactics are being overlooked. Those who are hurting blame God, get angry, and walk away. This is about the love of the Heavenly Father, and nothing and no one should be able to come between us and our Heavenly Father; especially not a fallen Christian. But Satan loves to use them to make others stumble and fall, as well. We all fall short but for the grace of God.

So think about it. If you believe God is so powerful that He could create everything, yet still believe He can't help you, then you need to check out a few Bible stories. You need to look at the stories of the people He protected, and those whom He was there for, no matter what. One thread of truth that runs through each story is the thread of faith. Each person showed faith and love for the Heavenly Father. These are the lessons that are put before us. We can learn from their examples.

When Esther went before the King to plead for her people, she did not say, "He probably won't give me favor." She believed her Uncle Mordecai when he said to her, "How do you know you were not born for this very moment?" But more than that, she had faith in her God. That is why she was able to say, "If I perish, I perish." (Esther 4:16 – KJV) Her life did not mean more to her than did her commitment and love for her omnipotent, awesome God.

Elisha and his servant were in a city surrounded by the enemy and the servant was in great fear, seeing that they were surrounded. But Elisha told the servant to "Fear not: for they that be with us are more than they that be with them." Then "Elisha prayed, and said, Lord, I pray thee, open his eyes, that he may see. And the Lord opened the eyes of the young man; and he saw: and, behold, the mountain was full of horses and chariots of fire round about Elisha." (II Kings 6:14-17 – KJV)

I truly believe we are in the Last Days, and I also believe the signs and wonders contained in the Book of Acts are nothing compared to what power God has planned to exhibit in the times ahead. If you sit in a dark room because someone just tripped over the light cord, you will be in the dark because of that person's tripping. But, if you get up, walk across the room and plug it back in, you will have power. The Lord died to provide us with access to His power and light, yet some would say that *He* made that person trip over the light cord. Therefore, they would blame God because they have no light.

But that is contradictory of what Jesus died for. He died because He loved us enough to trick Satan out of the keys to death and hell and give us eternal life. He actually gives us *three* keys to use but we often choose not to use them. Let me explain. Many people get angry with God and do not understand that if they would only use the Key of Knowledge, it would allow them to see into a situation clearly and truthfully. Then they could see and understand who is actually behind what has just happened to them and they wouldn't automatically blame God when bad things happen. The secret to knowledge is that it means you must wear the Belt of Truth and learn to recognize truth. A book that truly changed my life was *Telling Yourself the Truth*, by William Backus and Marie Chapian, for I learned much about recognizing the truth amidst the sea of lies that we encounter daily, and the truth really *will* set you free.

There are two other keys that the Bible speaks about that can give us more power in our lives. They are the Keys of Binding and Loosing. The Bible tells us of these keys in the New Testament: "And I will give unto thee the keys of the kingdom of heaven: and whatsoever thou shalt bind on earth shall be bound in heaven: and whatsoever though shalt loose on earth shall be loosed in heaven." (Matthew 16:19 – KJV) and again in Matthew 18:18, where it is reiterated, "Verily I say unto you, Whatsoever ye shall bind on earth shall be bound in heaven: and whatsoever ye shall loose on earth shall be loosed in heaven." (KJV)

There is a reason that these are called "keys" in the Bible. When you use your key, it unlocks a door. And who is it that said, "I am the door."? (John 10:9 – KJV) It is Jesus! He is the one who directs the angels, for it is not within our power to direct them. However if we use the keys He gave us to the door (Jesus), *He* will send those angels out with *His* assignments to help us. It is extremely important, however, that we use these keys carefully and properly when we pray. Too many people "bind and loosen" in their prayers without asking for knowledge; and therefore, their prayers may be for the opposite of what they are truly wishing to request.

My friend, Rabbi Barsky, gave me a simple explanation that I wish to share with you. When you pray, you should only bind that which you wish to *prohibit*. You should loose that which you wish to *permit*. These keys are powerful weapons, which God has placed at our disposal, so it is important that we read the Owner's Manual, His Word. Three Keys. One Door. What else do we need?

# Chapter
# 13

# *The Vision*

Sometimes it takes us longer to learn certain lessons than others. For me, that certainly seemed to be the case with marriage. The marriage to my third husband Jared was less than a year old and we were already fighting constantly. Convinced that everything was always someone else's fault, especially in this marriage, I believed I was only defending myself. But the demon Jealousy had a stronghold on me and that green-eyed monster played a larger part in my life than anyone knew. Jared was a gorgeous hunk of a man, but the fact that he was so handsome only fed my insecurity and made it impossible to sustain the relationship.

This particular night should have been no different from the many others that had preceded it. We had fought again and I decided to sleep on the couch. Still very angry and hurt, I was totally unprepared for the miraculous things that were soon to unfold.

At first I thought I had fallen asleep and was dreaming, because I could clearly see myself lying on the couch. But then everything became so real that I was convinced that I must be awake. I looked over at the window to see if the sun had risen and whether it was time to get up, but what I saw was unlike anything I could have ever expected.

The air outside the window was swirling with dust, like the dust storms often shown in movies. But usually that dust is brown. This dust was a deep orange. People were running up and down the street outside and they were screaming in terror. What could possibly be happening?

In an instant it struck me, like the proverbial light bulb coming on in my head. This is it!! This is the end of the world! Jesus has come back and we're not ready! Panic gripped my heart. I sat up but could not move from the couch. Fear kept me riveted in place. My gaze was pulled upward where the ceiling was being burned away, leaving a huge, gaping hole. Through the hole, the orange dust continuing to swirl in ever-thickening clouds. Then came the voice.

Out of the swirling dust storm, booming like thunder, came the words, **"THE TIME IS NOW!"**

I swallowed hard, trying not to choke on my fear and sat very still. Again came the thunderous voice, even louder than before: **"THE TIME IS NOW!"**

Pleading with the voice that could only be the voice of God Himself, I said, "Please Lord. Not yet. I'm not ready."

Yet a third time, the voice split the silence: **"THE TIME IS NOW!"**

Realizing that it was too late for me to do anything, I dropped my head into my hands and began to sob as never before.

After a time, there was silence. The voice had not spoken again. I slowly raised my head and looked over at the window. The light of early morning was streaming through. There was no more orange dust. There was no panic in the streets. The ceiling in my living room was back to normal, with no evidence of the fire that had burned it away earlier. Everything, it seemed, was back to normal, at least on the surface. I, however, would *never* be the same. This had been no dream. It was a vision of the end of time and I, like many others, wasn't ready.

People speak of the fear of the Lord, but what He had just shown me was the reality of what it would be like if He were to return this minute. It made me more aware than I had ever been in my life that I wasn't prepared. In fact, I wasn't even pursuing a path in that direction. I was attending church and I had accepted Christ as my Savior when I was nine; but like many people, I didn't give Him "me." The little girl that had said, "Yes, I will," to Christ had been doing her own thing for a long time now, and giving up control of my life, even to God, hadn't really been something to be considered.

Finally able to get up from the couch, I practically ran into the bedroom, trying to bury myself under the covers and hide next to my husband...anything to escape these awful feelings. As I lay there, a series of strange thoughts began to go through my mind. At that time, I did not understand how the Holy Spirit prompts us, but He was busy doing just that. *Answer the question,* He told me. *What do you think you're doing wrong?*

Searching my mind and finding only more questions, He then brought a starting place to my remembrance. "Remember the book you bought seven years ago in that Christian bookstore?" Then the Holy Spirit showed me the cover of the book. It had a picture of a man with puppet strings. Suddenly the title burst into my consciousness. It was *Doing Your Own Thing* by Bob Mumford. It had appealed to me because that's exactly what I wanted to do...my own thing. At that time, I was in the middle of a difficult divorce from my second husband, and did so want to find myself. After having had three babies and being a housewife for nine years, I felt I deserved a chance to find out who *I* was. The sad thing is, I never read the book. "You can read the book now," came that inner prompting again.

I began to argue that there was no way that book could be found now. After all, it had been seven years and I'd moved five times since then. I wouldn't even know where to look, I told myself, as I huddled down further under the covers.

"I'll show you." The thought had a commanding tone, as did the next two words: "Get up."

Determined now to prove the voice wrong, I got up, planning to just look around a little bit, justify the fact that the book couldn't be found, and go back to bed. But that is not what happened. We had a round table with storage underneath and I went straight to it, opened the doors. There under a pile of magazines was the book. I just sat there, staring at it, totally in awe of the moment. There are no words to adequately describe that feeling. Knowing that this was no coincidence, I sat down and began to read.

Amazed, I realized I was reading a version of my life. Doing your own thing didn't mean at all what I had thought it did when I purchased the book seven years ago. It was just the opposite. The more I read, the more apparent it became that I was more lost than I had ever been...all because I had been doing it *my* way. Between the vision and the insight gained from reading the book, I knew changes had to be made.

Change is not easy for anyone. There is a vast difference between coming to the realization that something is wrong and being able to do something about it. The Lord had placed me in a good, solid church with strong prayer warriors in my path. But since I hadn't really been paying attention, I was like a sixteen-year-old behind the wheel of an automobile for the first time. She knows that car has a steering wheel and brakes, but she hasn't got a clue how to use them properly. Still, she calls herself a driver. That was me.

I called myself a Christian, but didn't have a clear picture of what that meant in my life. There was so much for me to learn; yet I was too embarrassed to go to the people in the church for help. In fact, I didn't go anywhere. Consequently, I became very sick and had to quit my job. I sank into a deep depression and couldn't even drag myself out of bed. I just laid there day after day after day.

I probably would still be in that bed doing nothing, if it hadn't been for my good friend, Jody, who came to visit.

"If you think I'm going to continue to come here every day, visit you, bring chicken soup and pet and pamper you, you've got another 'thing' coming. So you might just as well get your butt out of that bed," she informed me.

With those words and her no-nonsense attitude, she blasted me right out of bed. I was so mad I had to get up. As I stood there fuming, it finally hit me. Sometimes you need chicken soup and sometimes you need a good swift kick in your behind to get you started. Jody was wise enough to know which one to deliver with love.

I started to move back into the land of the living and made some decisions that would take me forward. It would be safe to say that not all my decisions were the right ones, but they did get me back in motion. Divorce from Jared came less than one year after we married. Jared really was a good man. We just didn't invite Jesus into our marriage.

A job in Raleigh, North Carolina, offered me hope for a new start. Joseph stayed in Burlington with some family friends so that he could finish out high school there. I was determined to get to know my God and to get away from my problems. As time passed, He definitely taught me more about Himself, but somehow a lot of my problems had gotten in the car with me and moved right into my new home in Raleigh.

# Chapter
## 14

# Mother, Do You Know Who I Am?

As I recall, it was a gray, rainy day when I drove to visit my son, Joseph, who was then 15. It would take more than a few clouds to dampen my excitement about seeing my son. Joe was everything a mother could ask for in a son. He was a loving, respectful young man and was doing well in school. In fact, it was his keen sense of responsibility that sold me on the idea of allowing him to stay with a family I knew in Burlington so that he could complete his studies at his old high school. My company had just transferred me to Raleigh, and it was agreed that I would pay Joseph's room and board so that he could stay in Burlington until he graduated. Then he would be joining me in Raleigh. We had been through a lot together, Joseph and I, and I always looked forward to a chance to visit.

Joseph had called me in Raleigh and had asked me to come this time, saying that he needed to talk with me about something very important. I wasn't too concerned as I drove towards Burlington. After all, everything is important when you're fifteen.

When I arrived, Joseph surprised me by coming out of the house and meeting me at my car. Before I could get out, Joe slid into the passenger seat beside me. The look on his face was enough to tell me that something was definitely bothering him.

"I don't know how I'm going to tell you this, Mom," he finally said. "It's the hardest thing I've ever had to do."

Without even knowing what he wanted to discuss, I could see the anguish on his face and I just wanted to reach out with all my love and enfold him in it.

"Let me help you, son," I began, but in all honesty, there were very few things I could think of that could cause Joe to be this upset.

"Have you gotten some girl pregnant?" I blurted out, trying to spare my son the embarrassment of having to tell me.

"No. It's not that."

"Whatever it is, I can help you, Joseph." Not waiting for him to respond, I presented another possibility. "Is it drugs?"

"No. It's not drugs."

"Have you stolen something?"

"No, Mom. It's none of those things. Please stop guessing and listen."

"Well, those are the worst things that could happen," I continued, not really hearing his request to stop talking. "If it's anything else, it's nothing."

"I'm gay."

"Gay?" I asked in disbelief.

"Yes, Mother. That's what I needed to tell you."

My mind was racing. I was totally blind-sided. I didn't even comprehend what it meant to be gay. I couldn't even begin to find a way to respond. Finally, not wishing to offend my son by making judgments on something I basically knew nothing about; I asked Joe if we could please talk on Saturday. I would be coming back to Burlington then to pick him up and move him back home with me in Raleigh.

Ever so gently, he touched my shoulder and said, "I'm sorry, Mom. I know I have really hurt you," and with that, my eldest son got out of the car and walked back into the house. With those two words, "I'm gay," everything changed...and yet, nothing changed. My son's statement had opened my eyes to a different world, but it had not changed my deep love for my child.

I honestly don't know how I got back to Raleigh that night unless an angel drove my car. A torrential rain had made visibility poor and the driving conditions dangerous. As for me, I was beating the steering wheel with my fists and sobbing until my chest ached. I screamed out into the darkness.

"Why, God? I don't understand. I had such high hopes for this child. He has been a mother's dream from the moment that he was born. How could this happen? What can I do to stop this, Lord? It has to be fixed! It has to!" I had always felt that I had been able to fix things in my life before. I had been able to at least present the façade of being in control, but this...this was a whole new arena. I didn't even understand what it meant to be gay.

After I got back home, I began to search for answers. I began reading everything I could get my hands on that might help me understand what my son was going through, and who he was in terms of this new identity. I went to seminars and talked with counselors. And I prayed daily for my son. I educated myself about the gay lifestyle. I talked with my Heavenly Father and I talked with my son. I questioned how I could live with someone nearly sixteen years and never see a sign?

Then I thought about Jesus when he met Peter. Jesus saw Peter through eyes of love. Even though many people saw Peter as impetuous and perhaps not the most reliable person, Jesus saw Peter as a rock, a stable person. Jesus saw Peter's heart. I realized that I would always look at my son with eyes of love. I would not embrace his lifestyle decision, but I would continue to embrace my son.

I tried to think back, wondering if there were signs or something that I might have missed when Joseph was growing up. I felt as if I should have known. One thing that stood out was an incident that had happened while Joe was a Boy Scout.

I had enrolled Joseph in Boy Scouts so that he would have a strong father figure to observe. I wanted his world to include masculine role models, since his father would have nothing to do with him. I thought I was doing the right thing for my son.

Joseph's Boy Scout troop was going on a weekend camping trip. There were just five boys going and they were all excited. All the time he was gone, I thought about how much fun he must have been having. Soon it was Sunday and Joseph came home. He barely spoke as he came inside the house and then he went straight to bed. At the time, I didn't think much about it since when I was in the Girl Scouts and went camping, we stayed up almost all night telling ghost stories. It made sense that Joe was tired. But by mid-afternoon, he still hadn't gotten up, so I went into his room and sat on the side of his bed.

"Hey, sleepyhead. I've waited long enough to hear about this great camping trip."

"Oh Mom," he said weakly. "Just let me rest just a little while longer."

Thinking that he must have been more tired than I realized, I agreed to let him sleep some more and I left the room. It wasn't long before I began to feel very unsettled. I began pacing the floor and my spirit was jumping with an awareness that something was very wrong. I walked back in Joe's room.

"I've made your favorite, son...spaghetti," I coaxed, trying to sound more casual than I felt. "I'm ready to hear everything."

"It was really no big thing, Mom."

No big thing? This was his first camping trip and he had been so excited. Things were not adding up, so I decided to be more direct.

"One thing I do know, Joseph. You and I are very much alike when we're hurt. Sleep is our hiding place and we both know how to put ourselves into an almost coma state of sleep to escape pain. I'm your mother and I know you. I also know something must have gone very wrong on this trip."

"I can't talk about it, Mom," he responded, averting his eyes from mine.

"Son, do I keep any secrets from you? You know that my life is often a mess, but I don't hide anything from you. Whatever has happened, I can fix it. You can be assured of that."

"Mom, I know you believe you can fix anything, but you're not big and strong. You're just a frail little woman. There's no man in this house to protect you, and I couldn't stand it if you got hurt because of something I've done."

"Something *you* did? Okay, Joseph, will you trust me on one point here...just one? I want you to let me be the judge of whether you did something wrong. First of all, you're going to have to tell me what happened. Then, no matter what it is, I can promise you that we will work this through together."

"You have to promise me that you won't try to go after this man, Mother. He's big and he could hurt you."

Now fear struck my heart for the first time, but it was quickly replaced by a white hot anger as my child unraveled the cause of his pain.

"The first night we made a big campfire after we ate. The scoutmaster said we were going to play a game. He took one of the boys and went into the cabin while the rest of us were told to wait by the campfire. Then we heard yelling and crying coming from the cabin. Two of the guys went to see what was happening, but they didn't get very far. The scoutmaster came out and tied both of those boys to a tree for disobeying his game rules. Then he tied me and my other friend to another tree."

Joseph paused, and although I was trying to appear calm for my son's sake, I was shaking all over with rage.

Joseph saw how upset I was and quickly begged me not to go confront the scoutmaster.

"Promise me, Mom," he pleaded. "Don't go to this man's house. He knows where we live. He said he would hurt our families if any of us told what happened."

I reassured him as best I could, but this man had put a tremendous fear into my son.

"Try to put your mind at ease, Joseph. I will pray and God will handle this. You can be assured. God will show us what to do."

Joseph finally calmed down enough to go outside for a while, and I got on the phone with my boss. Since I had just moved to Raleigh, he was the only man I knew in the area.

"This is Toni, Mr. Wheeler," I told him when he answered the phone. "I'm calling to ask if you would mind coming in a little earlier tomorrow morning. I really need to talk to a man about something that has happened to my son this weekend."

"Sure, I'll be happy to help you if I can. How is eight-thirty in the morning?"

"That will be fine," I answered, grateful that he hadn't asked for details over the phone. "Thank you so much."

Mr. Wheeler prided himself on being on time, and by eight-thirty the next morning, I was sitting across the desk from him in his office. I began to tell him about the camping trip and I could see the muscles in his jaw tighten. He had two sons of his own, and he and I both knew that this could have happened to anyone's child. I had tried to keep myself calm, but I began to cry.

"He knows where I live, Mr. Wheeler, and he's threatened to hurt us if my son told what happened."

"Put your mind at ease, Toni. This can be handled in a way that he will never know that either you or your son has said anything. I don't think it's any coincidence that my best friend is the president of the Boy Scout Association for the entire state. I'm going to make a call to him right now. You just sit there and listen to the conversation.

As I listened, the two men planned a sting operation where the scoutmaster would be set up to take another group of boys camping. When he saw my concern, he assured me that this would be handled with law enforcement officers in the woods, and that the boys involved in the sting would be protected. No other children were going to be victims of this man. He assured me that the scoutmaster would be caught, and that he would have to pay the penalty for what he had done.

Mr. Wheeler was true to his word–the man was caught and punished. No other child would have to suffer because of that particular scoutmaster again.

We, as a society, have learned since then to talk more with our children, and to teach them about being wary of strangers and what is considered inappropriate touching. Joe grew up during a more innocent time. These things happened, I know, but people didn't talk about it. I'm certainly not saying all Boy Scout leaders, or any other person who works with children is automatically a predator; but our children need parents who are aware of the dangers that are out there and prepare their children. I know I wish I had, for I found out much later that this was not the only instance of molestation that Joseph had endured.

When he was eighteen, he finally told me about the other times. I found out that he had been molested at age five by a male babysitter, and again when he was seven or eight. The latter time, two men with a moving van had grabbed him while he was coming home from school. His route home took him down a lonely dirt road, and no one heard his cries as they pulled him into the woods, bound and gagged him, and sodomized him. Again, he told no one, hiding his bloody underwear and hurt body. If only he had told me then instead of waiting the nine years he had held this terrible secret inside. Those movers were working in the neighborhood that day and I could have traced the truck. The Lord says that vengeance is His and although I may never be able to confront them, I know in my heart that they won't go unpunished. They will have to answer to God Himself.

I was still trying to understand Joseph's announcement about being gay, and eventually, I asked Joseph to invite some of his friends in the gay community over to my apartment. I wanted to hear from them what it was like to be gay. I wanted to know how they felt, what they thought, and how they and their families were coping. I wasn't sure any of them would want to come but much to my surprise, seven of them showed up that night.

As soon as they had all settled themselves in my living room, I began to speak with them. I let them know how much I appreciated their coming to my home and being willing to help me understand. I also clearly stated that I meant no disrespect to them for their choice of lifestyle, but that my goal was to better understand my son. They allowed me to ask some very personal questions, and they actually seemed very anxious to talk to me. I found out that it had been very difficult for them to find non-judgmental people to talk to, so what I thought of as just an opportunity for me to come to a better understanding actually became an opportunity for them to be understood, as well.

Knowing that childhood molestation appeared to be a factor in Joseph's life, I needed to know if it might also have been a part of any of his friend's childhood experiences. Taking a deep breath, I asked them a difficult question.

"Have any of you ever been molested?"

All of them had, including my son. The time frames were between the ages of five and sixteen, and the incidences all varied from babysitters to uncles to strangers. Every one of them had kept this inside for some time before telling anyone, and some of them still had not told anyone before this night.

Not telling anyone seems to play an important part in Satan's work. He can do a lot with the secrets we hold inside. He can convince us that things others do to us, or we do to them, are normal. For example, our con-science may be pricked, and we may feel as if something is very wrong, but Satan is ready for that. He overpow-ers that feeling with *Don't think about it. It's just a nor-mal thing. After all, you're only human.* In short, Satan tells us lies as if they were truth and we believe him.

All of the young men in my apartment that night told of overbearing mothers, and absentee or non-involved fathers. There were definitely some common threads to their individual stories. My heart truly went out to each and every one of them. They were so sweet and kind to share their most private emotions with me. I felt I was-n't able to help them as much as they were helping me.

By now I was beginning to draw some conclusions. I am no doctor, but I have lived with the experience of having a gay child. I can assure you if I had it to do over, I surely wouldn't play into Satan's hands. It's my belief that a series of circumstances can make for an easy playing field for Satan's demon spirits. I don't think just an overbearing mother makes a gay child or just molestation, but a conglomeration of these things can surely set the groundwork. I never spoke with my child about not letting anyone violate his body or even talk suggestively to him. I didn't know how important this was so I put up no safeguards.

I wish I had let him know he could tell me anything, and that the lines of communication were always open to him. For whatever reason, that didn't happen. Joe kept silent and I believe with all my heart when a child can't confess something is wrong, the spirit world starts right then convincing them it's okay. That way, they can stop blaming themselves. The victim's initial reaction may be, "What did I do wrong? What did I do to cause this?"

But the lying spirit says, "Don't tell anyone. You did-n't do anything wrong. It's normal for man to lay with man. You were born that way."

By now, I could see that I had the undivided attention of Joe and his friends, so I just kept going.

"Let me tell you a story to illustrate what I mean," I continued. "It's a story about a farmer and a field, and it's something that the Lord showed me. He showed me how a farmer selects just the right field for the crop he intends to grow. Some crops require much sun, some require a lot of moisture, some require afternoon shade. Each of these things is taken into consideration as the farmer chooses his field. After he chooses the field, he then prepares it. He plows the ground so it will provide a good place for the seed to grow. Then and only then, does he plant the seed and wait for the harvest.

"In similar fashion, when Satan wants to plant an idea, he does the same thing. He looks for the best place for his crop to grow. Several of you tonight said you were born this way and that's all there is to it. I challenge you to look at that thought another way. I want you to look at it as a seed planted by Satan to confuse your thinking. In the case of you young men here tonight, some of the fields Satan chose were those with an overbearing mother, an absentee father or childhood molestation. Into this fertile ground he planted the seed of misconception. The seed he planted grew into a belief system that you all seem to have expressed in one way or another. You've told me that you shouldn't feel guilty, for after all, you were born this way. But I challenge you to consider that Satan used you, betrayed you and lied to you.

"These are only my thoughts, but I would like to make a statement. First, let me preface. I am NOT saying all gay children came from parents like me. I thank God for repentance. Before we can repent, we must see the real error, just as the Lord sent the prophet to David, so he sent many people to me. I believe when a man and woman marry and conceive a child, there is a Godly protection for that small baby. But I also believe we have

117

doorways that can be opened through sin and that Satan takes each opportunity we give him and strategically plans his battle.

"If we open the door, we give Satan, the accuser of the brethren, the right to hurt us in any way he chooses; in our health, our finances, or our children. The doorway I opened started when Joseph was in my womb. It hurts me to tell you this, but I feel I must. If I can really help just one mother to save her child, I must share this story.

"I was pregnant with Joseph at the same time one of my girlfriends was also pregnant, and we had been out shopping together for baby things. We had gone by her parents' home for her to pick up something and I waited for her in the foyer. When she returned, I asked her about the large pictures of men on the foyer wall.

"'They are my brothers,' she said.

"'Well, that one is mine,' I said, pointing to the youngest.

"'Brad? He's getting married Sunday, and have you forgotten that you're already married and expecting a baby? You're too late.'

"'No, I'm not,' I said, more determined than ever. 'He's mine.' The word was out all over town that my husband, Danny, was stepping out on me. In fact, just the night before I said these fateful words. We had had a big fight, and Danny had kicked me in the stomach. I was primed by Satan again, and so it was not surprising that I was already planning another escape.

"I believe my child was marked as fair game for Satan at this moment. Just as David looked at Bathsheba as she bathed on her roof, his heart was set to have her. It's our heart the Lord is after and it is our heart that Satan would try to steal. 'As a man thinketh, so is he.' (Proverbs 23:7 – KJV)

"I had a beautiful, kind, precious little boy growing inside me, and I allowed danger to come around him as surely as if I had laid him on a park bench and walked away. I'm not surprised to hear you tell me tonight that you were born that way. I believe that Satan went after my unborn child while he was still inside me. I did have the affair and I did mess up a lot of lives, including my own. Satan looks at what we value, and that's what he goes after.

"David didn't value money. He valued Bathsheba and her child. Satan used that open door to try to turn David against God. A generational curse is one that is passed down, but each person has a choice to accept that generational curse or overcome it. All types of addiction fall under the heading of generational curses. But there is a point of decision that we *all* come to. It is the point where free will either compels us to repent and break it for ourselves, or accept the curse as an inevitable legacy.

"The way I see it, love is the key that can unlock the door. But if a parent rejects a gay child, they have already lost because they have chosen to not even be in the game. When we sin, we allow Satan to pick his target. It may be our children, our family, our health, our finances, etc. People think that when they sin they only put themselves in jeopardy. This is one of Satan's greatest lies. He doesn't want us to know that sin opens all kinds of doors and that once we open them, Satan can walk right in.

"I don't stand here and condemn you tonight. Understand that clearly. I cannot condone this lifestyle choice, but I love my son and I know God loves my son. I also know that God loves each and every one of you. What I cannot do and God will not do is decide for you. You have a free will.

"I want you to know that you are always welcome in my home, as long as you respect my right to not agree with your choice. You are my son's dearest friends, and I want you to feel welcome here. I will be here to listen if any one of you needs me. That's pretty much all I have to say and I really do appreciate your courtesy of listening to me and coming over here."

I stood there wondering just how all I had said had been received. I really wanted it to be a night of mutual understanding. I soon got my answer as each of the young men came up and hugged me, and thanked me for caring about them enough to invite them to my home. I knew they would be back, and they knew they would be welcome.

# Chapter
# 15

# *The Bargain*

With three marriages now behind me, I was finally beginning to get on my feet. Joseph was with me, and I was learning day by day to seek God's will in more and more areas of my life. This is not to say that I had turned my life around in an instant. Nothing could be further from the truth. I still had many of Satan's strongholds within me that would have to be identified and overcome, but I was taking my first steps towards spiritual freedom.

Right then, my primary goal was to try to gain custody of my son, Bryan. Two years ago, Brad had married again for the third time. His new wife wanted Brad to herself, and made it quite clear that she felt that Bryan was not part of the picture. Partially at her insistence, and partially due to Bryan's defiant resistance to his new situation, she decided that Bryan needed to be sent away to a camp for difficult children. I disagreed and fought against it. Brad was no help at all as he basically took instructions from his new wife.

In fact, one time on the phone with me she had bragged about how she wore the pants in that family. I called the camp to try to get Bryan released to me, but every possible avenue had been blocked by Brad with court orders. I had legal visitation rights and the court papers to back it up, but somehow, no one seemed to care. And I was turned away again and again.

In my despair, I found myself making a bargain with God. Oh, how much I still had to learn about how God works.

I prayed earnestly to my Heavenly Father, "Lord, I've been to court once to get custody, and lost because the court saw that I didn't own a home or have a husband and that my job, which requires me to cover five states, keeps me away a lot. Brad had remarried and his wife was at home, so for that reason the court thought it would be better for Bryan to live with his father. But Lord, You know that I am a good mother. I take good care of Joseph in spite of my job and the fact that I'm a single mother. I know I could work it out for Bryan, too. So I'm pleading with You, Father. Please prepare the way for my son to be returned to me."

At this point I set forth the terms of my request.

"I have one thousand dollars from an income tax refund, Father. I'll put it in a savings account until I can find a good lawyer. I know I will win with You on my side. Oh...and I promise that I will be THE BEST MOTHER You have ever seen. I will raise my children in a Godly home. I will stay out of bars and any other places that You would not have me go. I'll be home with my children as much as I can. I will be such a good mother if You will only help me get my son back. Please, God!"

I had presented what I felt was a fair and honest con-tract with God. I'll do my part and God will do His. I was about to learn that no bargain can be made with a God of grace. What I didn't realize at the time was that there was nothing I could do or say that would entice God to help me. He would help me regardless of what I did. All I had to do was ask and realize His ways are higher than our ways. "And it shall come to pass, that before they call, I will answer, and while they are yet speaking, I will hear." (Isaiah 65:24) When He does what He does, He does it His way.

About four o'clock the same afternoon, my telephone rang. A friend of mine who lived near Brad was calling to tell me that Bryan had returned home from Camp Callwood. Only nine when he had been sent there, Bryan was now approaching eleven, and I was quite sure that the camp had not helped this troubled child. I was also sure that, given the chance, my love and God's power could heal his emotional wounds. I truly believed that love and a home is all any child really wants. Suddenly, knowing that Bryan was so very close to me, I was determined to try one more time to see him. After all, I had the legal right to see him, and that was exactly what I was going to demand. Once again I placed the visitation papers in my pocketbook and worked on a plan of action. The next day, I would put it in operation.

"Joseph," I said to my eldest son when he came home that day, "I need you to stay home from school tomorrow."

"Why? I'm not sick."

"I know, Son, but I need your help. I'm going to ask Brad to let me bring Bryan and Steven here for the weekend. I intend to try to see Bryan first, then ask Brad if I can take them for the weekend. I'm sure that Brad and his wife have told Bryan I don't love him or want him. I'm also pretty sure that he's going to be very angry that I did not rescue him from Camp Callwood. He doesn't even know that I tried. He may not want to talk to me at all. That's where you come in, Joseph. I'm really depending on you to tell him that they were lying to him, that I've tried my best to see him and to have him with me. It won't be easy, Son."

"We can do it, Mom. When do you want to leave?"

"I want to get there before school is out because I think my best opportunity to see him is by going straight to the principal and asking to take him out of school early. It's going to be a tough time, I know. Bryan is bound to be angry with me."

The next afternoon, Joseph and I arrived at the school about thirty minutes before the buses were to leave to take the children home. The principal was a former acquaintance of mine who knew me from the volunteer work I had done in the community when I was president of the Retarded Children's Association. But the look on the principal's face as I entered his office was not reassuring, and I quickly understood that there was going to be a problem.

"I'd like to take my son, Bryan, out of school early today," I stated calmly. "I've just arrived in town and I've not seen him since he came home from Camp Callwood. Would you please get him for me?"

The principal looked at me briefly, then lowered his head.

"I wish I could do this for you, Toni. But I can't. Brad has put it on the school records that you're not allowed to pick him up. He's even asked that you be kept off the school grounds."

Beginning to cry, I pleaded with him. "I have legal visitation papers. I've not seen my son in a year-and-a-half. This just isn't right. Please, help me."

The principal looked up at me, compassion obviously showing on his face.

"Toni, I know that you are a good woman, but my hands are tied legally. You see that water fountain down at the end of the hall?" he asked pointing out through his open office door.

124

"Yes, I see it ," I answered, puzzled by his apparent change of subject.

"Well, I'm really thirsty and if you will excuse me, I'm going down there to get a drink of water. I'll have to leave these bus schedules on my desk, but I'll be right back to talk with you."

As the principal left the room to get his water, my eyes dropped to his desk. Right in front of me were the bus schedules, just as he had said. It was a God-given opportunity. Quickly I scanned the pages and found Bryan's name. Now I knew the bus number and the location of the bus stop where he would be dropped off. I had just returned the list to the principal's desk when he returned. I thanked him for his time and told him that, while I didn't agree with it, I understood his position. I then excused myself as quickly as possible and left, joining Joseph in the car.

"We've got a chance now," I exclaimed, and quickly explained to Joseph what had happened in the school.

I let Joseph off at Bryan's bus stop, and watched as he hid himself behind some trees and brush so he would not be seen before Bryan got off the bus. I pulled around the corner and parked in front of a house in an adjoining neighborhood. Anxiously, I waited.

A knock on the car's window startled me.

"Excuse me, Miss, but I need to ask you what you're doing here. We have a Neighborhood Watch and we've noticed you just sitting here," she said as she gestured to several other women standing together on a nearby lawn.

I got out of my car and explained the situation. My whole body was shaking from the emotional impact of all that had happened so far. As she stood there with me, she patted me on the shoulder in a comforting fashion

125

and said, "Stay as long as you like. You'll be safe. We're all Christians and we will be praying for you."

After what seemed like an eternity, Joseph came into sight. Bryan was at his side. My heart leapt with joy. I hadn't been sure Joseph would be able to get Bryan to listen to him. Tears of joy began to stream down my face.

The boys were closer now, and I could see how thin and frail Bryan looked. Still crying with joy, I ran toward my sons. At about the same time, Bryan caught sight of me and ran to meet me. There we stood; a mother and her two boys locked in a three-way embrace in the middle of the street. The Neighborhood Watch lady and the other mothers who had been watching and praying, dabbed at their now-wet eyes, and turned to go into their own homes, leaving the three of us to our private reunion.

"They told me you hated me, Mother. They said you never loved me. Why didn't you write? Why didn't you call?"

"I tried, Son. I really did. At the camp and at the school, I was turned away. I wrote, but they must have kept my letters from you. Oh, how I wish I could have saved you from all the pain."

The look on Bryan's face told me more than words that he forgave me.

I decided it would be best if the two boys went to Brad's by themselves and let him know I was in town. I assured the boys that I would go to a pay phone and call Brad after they had had time to tell him. I held my breath as I watched the two of them walk out of sight.

I paced nervously in front of a pay phone for about twenty minutes. The boys should have had time to get there and let him know by now, I reasoned. With trembling fingers, I dialed Brad's number. I only intended to ask if Bryan could spend the weekend with me.

An outraged Brad answered the phone.

"I knew you'd eventually pull some stunt like this. It's a good thing I came home from work early today."

"I just want to have my son visit, Brad. That's not asking much, and I do have the legal right to see him."

"I couldn't care less about your legal rights. He wants to come *live* with you, and frankly, I 'm fed up. I'm through with him. You need to get over here right now and get him."

I was filled with panic. I had certainly not anticipated this. I had been prepared for a visit, but not for full custody...not immediately, at least. All the barriers to such an arrangement, such as my job travels, Joseph's still being in school, and so on, flooded my mind.

"Please, Brad," I pleaded. "Just let him visit and I'll get things worked out to take him for good soon. I just need a little time to prepare. You've taken me by surprise."

"And your little scheme hasn't taken me by surprise? Look. I'm not asking you, I'm telling you. Get over here and get him RIGHT NOW!"

I knew this might be my only chance.

"I'm coming! I'll take him! Tell him I'm coming!"

I threw down the receiver and dashed to my car. As I turned into the driveway, Joseph came running out of the house.

"He's got a loaded gun, Mom. Stay in the car."

Brad and Bryan came walking out with a huge cardboard box with what I assumed were all of Bryan's belongings. Actually, I would find out later, it only contained one shirt and one pair of jeans. Despite Joseph's warning, I had gotten out of the car and faced Brad and Bryan as they approached the driveway. Brad dropped the box at my feet and said menacingly, "You have sixty seconds to take this kid and get out of here. I never want to see either one of you ever again!"

I looked at him with disbelief. "You can't mean that. This is your son. How can you act this way in front of the children?"

"I'll show you," Brad yelled as he whirled around and ran back into the house.

I grabbed up the box, which was large enough to have held a 25" TV, and tried to stuff the unwieldy carton into the back seat of the car. My hands were shaking so much I could not get it in. Joseph came around to help just as Brad came out of the house with a rifle in his hand.

"You've got sixty seconds, Toni. Take that brat and go. You will never see Steven again and live." Steven was holding on to my skirt and Brad jerked him away and commanded him to go in the house.

Brad leveled the rifle at my head and I froze momentarily. I could see his wife looking out the window with a look of sheer delight on her face, but still I could not move. Joseph ran up behind me and hit me behind the knees, caught me, and pulled me to the passenger's side of the car. Pushing me in, he grabbed the car keys and stuffed the box into the trunk before climbing in behind the wheel. With Bryan in the back, Joseph began to back out of the driveway. Tears of disbelief and terror were rolling down my face as I called out to Brad one last time: "Brad, how can you do this to your children? I just don't know you anymore!"

Joseph drove quickly away from Brad's house and the three of us rode in silence for a short distance. Finally, I composed myself enough to remember that Joseph, who was just barely fifteen, didn't even have a license to drive. I had Joe pull over and I took over driving. Bryan asked to get in the front seat and Joe said it was okay with him. I was still somewhat in shock and still about thirty minutes from my apartment when I glanced over and looked at Bryan sitting in the front seat beside me. It was then that it finally hit me. The bargain with God!

I began to laugh and both boys looked at me wondering, I'm sure, what I could possibly have to laugh about.

But I knew. I hadn't had to go to court. God didn't need my thousand dollars. He didn't need my plan. He had one of His own.

As I looked over at Bryan, I knew he had been returned to me by a merciful, giving God who had heard me crying in the wilderness and reached down to help. My heart was about to burst with joy and thanksgiving.

# Chapter
# 16

# *Transitions*

*F*inally, we were a family again. I could hardly believe what had happened in less than twenty-four hours. I had gone from a mother longing for her son in her heart to a mother with that same son in her home and her arms. I was determined to let Bryan know how glad I was to have him with us. I planned and prepared a special welcome home dinner. I had always loved to cook, but I seldom gave myself time to enjoy it. Today would be different. It seemed that every aroma in the kitchen was intensified. The colors of the lettuce and tomatoes seemed brighter. The kitchen seemed to be filled with light and life. I prepared fried chicken, creamed potatoes, two of Bryan's favorites, and a special dessert that both the boys loved. This was going to be a celebration!

As the boys came through the door, I handed them each a plate. "It's all laid out on the counter. Take whatever you'd like."

As I watched, I noticed that Bryan wasted no time in filling his plate; in fact, I wasn't sure everything was going to stay on his plate, he had heaped his food so high. *I'm glad he likes what I cooked,* I thought. I quickly filled my plate and had just sat down next to Joseph when I noticed Bryan. He was attempting to bring a glass of milk back to the table with him but he had poured the glass so full that it was sloshing over the rim of the glass as he walked.

"What are you doing, Bryan?" Joseph asked.

"What do you mean? Have I done something wrong?" Bryan asked. His frightened tone took me by surprise.

"Not wrong, exactly," said Joseph. "But you've got to admit it's pretty ridiculous to fill your glass so full that it spills out when you carry it. You should know that you can go back to the refrigerator and get more if you want it."

"I can?" Bryan responded, incredulously.

"Of course, you can," I told him. "Why would you ever think you couldn't?"

"When I was in that camp, we were only allowed one glass of liquid and I learned to fill it up to the brim because that's all we would get to drink."

"Bryan! I can't believe it. What kind of a place were you in?"

As Bryan sat down, he began to tell us of the experiences he had endured at Camp Callwood.

"On my very first day there, two years ago, I was standing in the lunch line, waiting to get my plate. I was feeling pretty sad and alone and I really didn't understand why I was there in the first place. Suddenly, five other boys yanked me out of line and out the door. They started hitting me, and I started hitting back, but there were five of them and I got, by far, the worst of it. They knocked me down and held my face in the snow. See this line on the side of my cheek? That's frostbite.

"Finally a counselor came over and broke up the fight, but to my surprise, he blamed me. 'I heard you were fighting a lot in your last school and I see you're

132

fighting here, as well,' he said. 'In case you think you might want to fight any more, just let us know and we can certainly accommodate you.' He never said anything to the five boys who had beat me up. Later I learned that the counselor had put the guys up to it to keep me in line from day one. I guess it worked," Bryan sighed, sounding defeated. "I didn't fight any more after that day."

I sat stunned by what I had just heard. My son had not been sent to a place of healing. He had been sent to people who tried to break his spirit. He had been hungry and no one had cared. He had been hurt and no one had comforted him. The "safe place" his father had sent him had not been a safe place at all.

That night, when I checked on Bryan after putting him to bed, I was surprised to find him sleeping, not on the bed but on the floor with his face close to the air vent. Waking him gently, I asked, "Son, why don't you sleep in your bed?"

"I got used to sleeping on the floor at Camp Callwood, Mom. But I really sleep down here because I can't breathe in the bed."

"Can't breathe?" I exclaimed. "Why ever not?"

"I haven't been able to breathe well since I had the accident with the swing at Dad's and that was before I went to the camp. I never saw a doctor or anything."

I sat down suddenly on the bed. I believed that if I heard even one more shocking word from this child, it would cause me to fall to the floor myself.

Monday morning I called a doctor to assess Bryan's breathing problem.

After examining Bryan, the doctor turned his attention to me. "Just who is this child's parent?" he demanded.

"He's my son," I began, "but I just got custody of him this weekend. He's been in the custody of his father and stepmother prior to that."

"And they let him live like this?"

"I don't understand. What's wrong with Bryan?"

"His nose was crushed in that swing accident. Do you understand? His nose was crushed into the cavity of his face and it's a wonder he can breathe at all."

I could barely manage to speak as the enormity of what my child had been through washed over me. All that time at camp he was in pain from an accident he had before he was even put in the camp.

"Can you fix it?" was all I could manage.

"It can be done, but it's expensive."

"Whatever it takes," I heard myself say. "Whatever it takes."

"I think we should do the surgery immediately," the doctor stated. "He's suffered too long already."

"Of course. When can..." I began, only to have the doctor interrupt.

"Have him here tomorrow morning at seven," the doctor replied. Turning to Bryan, he patted him encouragingly on the shoulder. "What do you say, Champ? Shall we fix that nose?"

"Yes, sir," replied Bryan. "Yes, sir."

After surgery the next day, it was a triumphant doctor who emerged from the O.R. to greet me. "It's amazing, really. There were only fragments to work with, but we actually sewed fragments together to rebuild his nose. He'll be able to breathe just fine from now on."

"Can I see him?" I inquired.

"He's still pretty groggy, but you can certainly sit with him if you'd like."

"Thank you, doctor. Thank you so much."

I sat by my sleeping child who, despite the swelling from surgery, appeared to be doing fine. I began to ponder the mysterious ways in which my God works.

My mind floated back to that day in the courtroom when I first lost custody of Bryan. "A safe, stable home environment," that judge had said. Yet here in front of me was the evidence that a safe and stable home environment had not been what Bryan had been given. It broke my heart to realize the torture this child had been through, the neglect, the loneliness.

Just as I had been placed in danger by a parent who thought she was "protecting her child," so Bryan had been abandoned to abuse in what should have been a safe haven. I may never know exactly what measures God took in behalf of my child, but I am sure that He preserved Bryan's life for a purpose. Two generations, growing up years apart, yet enduring such similar childhood experiences. Now was the time to start learning about generational curses. I knew in my heart I was reaping the consequences of my actions. "Fools because of their transgression, and because of their iniquities, are afflicted." (Psalms 107:17 – KJV) In other words, God does **NOT** put hurt on you. Your transgressions afflict you. I can testify to this.

# Chapter
# 17

# The Bag Lady

The reality of having Bryan with me after so many years of separation was quite different from what I had expected. I found I was quite unprepared for the presence of a third person in my tiny apartment. Shortly after Bryan's surgery, I knew we would have to find a larger place to live. Although I made a decent salary at that time, it didn't seem to go as far as it had before. Since none of the fathers of my children would so much as buy them a pair of shoes, let alone pay child support, finding a larger place would mean budgeting more carefully. But God's marvelous provision just kept pulling me out. I hadn't had to go to court to get custody of Bryan, and the thousand dollars I had set aside for the attorney was still in my savings account. That would cover a security deposit and the first month's rent, at least. After that, I would have to map out a very careful financial strategy.

I was surprised and pleased at how quickly I was able to find new living accommodations. I had taken a week's vacation from my job; and by the end of the week, the boys and I were moved in, if not settled in, to our new home.

Bryan had been with me for a month, and I had managed to juggle my schedule so that I could see clients close enough to home so that I would not have to be gone overnight. But I couldn't escape the fact that my territory now covered five states, and I knew I was going to have to travel overnight again.

It was about sunrise on a Saturday morning when I found myself sitting in the den, gazing out the window without really seeing anything. "Lord," I asked. "What am I going to do? I am so grateful to have Bryan with me, but I can't believe that You would allow him to come home with Joseph and me, and not give me a way to take care of him. Lord, I'm asking for a miracle. I don't have any more money. I have to work. I can't leave my boys alone. Lord, I'm lost and I'm afraid. Please. Show me. What shall I do?"

I stared aimlessly out the window after I concluded my prayer. As I continued to gaze out the window, I thought I heard a voice. It was more like a whisper actually, softly intruding into my thoughts. I turned, but no one was there. But then I heard it again. This time I knew I had heard a voice and I stopped to listen more carefully.

"Why don't you look at one of those papers?" came the prompting. "Look at the want ads."

Papers? What papers? Then I remembered a pile of yellowed newspapers that the previous residents had left heaped on the porch. I had intended to throw them away for over two weeks, but something had always seemed more important. Those must be the ones.

"Now that would be foolish," I argued. "If there was anyone any good in there, someone would have snatched them up by now."

I walked into the kitchen, poured myself a cup of coffee and was walking back to the den when I glanced out the window and saw the papers. Again the voice prompted me.

"Oh, what would it hurt to look? At least you would be doing something."

I opened the front door and approached the pile of papers. I grabbed up a stack and took them back into the den. I selected one at random and opened it to the want ads. It was over three weeks old and yellowed from the sun's beating in on the porch. Surely, there were no answers to my prayers in papers that should have gone into the trash weeks ago, but like the voice had said, at least I would be doing *something*.

*Here's one*, I thought. Housekeeper wants job. Call Rennee. 555-7346. *Well, I'm not going to call that one*, I decided. She says she wants a job, not a place to live. Just about that time, my phone rang. I laid the paper down and forgot about it for the time being.

It was that same day that I found out I would have to do a press run in Baltimore, Maryland, and I would have to be out of town for two or three days. I needed somebody to care for the boys *now*. I didn't know what to do. I couldn't lose my job and I couldn't leave my children. Glancing at the papers I had left in the den, I decided that I had nothing to lose by calling on that housekeeper ad.

Rennee answered the phone. I don't remember much of the conversation, but she indicated that she wanted fifty dollars a week. I certainly knew that this was more than fair, but I had to tell her that I couldn't even afford that, and I never mentioned the possibility of her living with us. Feeling quite defeated, I hung up the phone.

"Why didn't you tell her you have two children and get no child support?" The prompting voice had not left me.

"What good would that do? She needs fifty dollars a week, and I don't have it," I said out loud as I headed for bed, where I spent a very restless night.

When I got to my Raleigh office on Monday, it was clear that everything had been put in place for my trip to Baltimore, and I couldn't get out of it. I didn't know what I was going to do.

When I got home that afternoon, I was sick with worry. I slumped in my old blue chair and leaned my head back in frustration.

"Lord, I don't know what to do. I've asked for Your help and I feel You must be trying to help me. Am I blocking You in some way? This is going to take a miracle, and You have shown me miracles before. Help me, Father. I don't know what to do." Tears began to roll down my face as I sat there in silence.

"Call Rennee," the voice prompted. "I will give you the words to say."

"I'm not even going to argue this time," I said. "What have I got to lose?" I dialed Rennee's number.

Rennee answered, "Hello."

"Hi. I'm the lady who called you Saturday. If you've got a minute, I would like to tell you my story, and then see if you and I could work something out." She agreed to listen. After I was honest about my predicament and my desperate need for help, I then presented my offer. I would give Rennee free room and board and twenty-five dollars a month spending money to begin with. She could buy her personal items with the grocery money, and I would see that she had clothes if she needed them. I told her I would raise her salary as I got raises. I knew it wasn't the best deal in the world, but it was all I could offer.

"Yes," she said immediately.

Now I was on guard, wondering what was wrong with her. I know it was awful to think that; but I also knew I wasn't offering her a good deal, and I was suspicious that she would agree to it so readily. I would have to see what she was like for myself, so I told her that I wanted to drive over and meet her. She gave me directions and I set off to interview our new housekeeper. As I approached the neighborhood where Rennee lived, I began to feel a bit uneasy with the surroundings, but I had promised to meet this woman and I was determined to keep my word.

As I pulled the car over at the address Rennee had given me, there was a young woman standing in the yard. Her appearance was very unkempt, and I was really taken aback when she got into the car to talk with me. What I was to find out was that her need was as great as mine.

Her parents had kicked her out of the house when she was thirteen, and she had lived with an aunt for a while. By the time she was fifteen, the mistreatment she had endured became too much; she joined the ranks of the homeless and became a bag lady on the streets of Chicago. That is where she was living when the man she called her "boyfriend" found her. He brought her to North Carolina with promises of a better life, but what he did was something entirely different.

Her boyfriend pulled his trailer up behind a house belonging to his new girlfriend. With no place to go and no money to leave, Rennee was forced to stay. She had to watch the man she had come to love and trust while they were in Chicago give all his attention to another woman now that they were in North Carolina. She was told she would have to "earn her keep," as her boyfriend put it. Nobody was going to live with him for free. Much to Rennee's horror, she found that he intended that she earn it through prostitution. When Rennee refused, he beat her. She refused again, and he threatened to kill her. Knowing that he meant it, she relented. He took all her money and kept her as a virtual slave.

One morning, Rennee woke up to find that her boyfriend had hitched up his trailer and left, taking everything Rennee owned with him. The woman who owned the house gave Rennee the use of a bedroom in an unheated part of her home, but required Rennee to do all the housework and wait on her in exchange.

As Rennee finished speaking, I looked intently at her again. What I saw, however, was not the same Rennee who originally climbed into my car. In a split second, I saw Rennee as God saw her. Nothing about Rennee had changed, really. Yet, through the grace of God, how she appeared on the outside is not what I saw. Instead I saw a lonely heart begging for acceptance. I saw a person with infinite potential and unlimited possibilities. I was allowed to see beyond the surface, and focus on the true worth of Rennee as a person as God revealed it to me. It was the first time I remember being aware of this happening, but God knew it would not be my last.

It was clear that Rennee was desperate. She needed me as much as I needed her. Despite all I had heard, I truly believed that she was the person God had sent me and I agreed to come back for her the next day.

"Bring a truck," she said. "I do still have a few things."

As Joseph and I pulled up with the truck the next day, Rennee was again standing by the road, waiting. It was a good thing we brought a big truck because obviously Rennee did still have quite a few things left after her boyfriend "stole everything she owned."

"You've got to be kidding," Joe said as he looked at her.

Rennee was about my age, but it was obvious that the years had taken their toll on her. Actually, she looked worse than the day before. I chided myself for not preparing Joe for her appearance. Her hair was down past her shoulders; the bottom half of it was as red as fire, and the upper half, from her ears up was graying and almost white. Her hair was so thin on top that she looked as if she were almost bald. It was obvious that her hair had not been washed in weeks, as it was all stuck together. She had on a pair of plaid polyester pants and a striped shirt. Her socks were mismatched and she was wearing sandals over her socks. She wore no make-up and her teeth had a decidedly greenish tinge.

"Do you really want to go through with this?" Joe asked. "It isn't too late to back out. She's unbelievable, Mom!"

"I'll clean her up," I told him. "I can do it. You'll see. Give me one week and you won't even know it's the same person. Joe, please try to understand. I need her and I know she needs me."

"Okay," Joe said, shaking his head in disbelief. "Mom, you never cease to amaze me."

# Chapter
# 18

# *The Transformation*

*I* really didn't have any idea what I was getting myself into. I found I was totally unprepared for what a horrendous time we would have trying to adjust to each other. Rennee absolutely refused to let anyone touch her hair, and she wouldn't agree to taking a bath, either. In spite of this, she turned out to be an immaculate housekeeper. Both my children thought I was playing a joke on them. I don't think it occurred to me to prepare them for how she looked, because what I saw in Rennee was quite different from what they saw.

Bryan made fun of her and gave her a hard time from minute one. She would fix his breakfast and he wouldn't eat it. He didn't want her in his room because he insisted that she "moved things." Finally I had to confront the issue of her appearance.

"Rennee, if you want to keep living here, you're going to have to take a bath and wash your hair, and then do something about your wardrobe. I think we're about the same size and...."

"A bath?" Rennee interrupted. "I don't need a bath."

"Let me assure you, Rennee. You definitely do."

"Well, I don't like them," Rennee stated firmly.

"If you're going to work for me, Rennee, you're going to be clean. Besides, I'll guarantee you've never had a bath like I have planned for you."

"I...I don't know," Rennee responded, and I could see her resolve not to bathe was slipping.

"Come with me. We're going to fill the tub with warm water and lots of bubble bath. We'll surround the tub with candles, dim the lights and play some soft, relaxing music. It will be such a luxury, you'll want to have one every night."

"Bubble bath? Candles? That's not a bath. That sounds more like a party."

"It can be, if you make it one, Rennee. How you take your bath is up to you. I'm only telling you to take one...and while you're in there you'll find a brand new toothbrush that I bought for you, so please brush those teeth."

Rennee finally agreed and later told me about the sheer delight of the experience as the bubbles tickled her nose and the candles flickered a relaxing glow around the room. While Rennee was finding out just how wonderful cleaning up could feel, Joseph came home.

Joe and I were talking over a cup of coffee when Rennee came into the room. She smelled of roses from the bubble bath, and she looked much better in my shirt and jeans than she had in the outfit she had been wearing before. Her hair was wrapped up in a towel, turban-style, but a tear shone brightly in her eye, just about to drop.

"Rennee, you look great! But why are you about to cry?"

"I'm so very happy, but I'm also pretty upset."

"What has you upset?"

146

"My hair."

"Your hair? Why?"

"I washed it three times and I used some of that fancy conditioner stuff you left in there, but they won't come out."

"What won't come out?" I asked.

"All these tangles," Rennee whimpered. "Just look."

Rennee swept the towel turban off her head and her long hair dropped unceremoniously about her shoulders. It was evident she had tried to comb out the snarls, but the hair was matted in so many places that it was impossible.

"Joseph, would you call Michael and see if he can come over and help out with this?"

"Who's Michael?" Rennee asked.

"Michael is a friend of Joseph's who's one of the best hair stylists in town. We'll take care of this. Don't worry."

Michael arrived about a half hour later and while I prepared supper, Michael attempted to salvage what he could of Rennee's hair.

I went to call everyone to supper and found myself stopping at the doorway. Rennee had her back to me at first but then turned slowly and shyly towards me. Michael had gotten rid of her flaming red and white hair by applying a soft flattering shade of hair color, and had cut her hair into a short swinging bob that flattered her delicate features. Rennee's eyes were bright with excitement and she flashed a wide smile, revealing teeth that now sparkled.

"How do I look?"

"Breathtaking," I replied honestly. "It's a wonderful transformation. Come on, everybody. You too, Michael. You've definitely earned your supper tonight."

It soon became clear that Rennee was the perfect person for us. The boys were won over by her friendliness and her specialty pizza, and I could now come home to a house that was already cleaned and welcoming. Rennee began to get hugs from the kids and lots of praise for the good things she was doing. She really did save me money in lots of ways. She had grown up being thrifty, and her habit of saving things often paid off. I remember one time in particular that the boys and I still joke about. Rennee had saved all the plastic wrappings from everything we bought and had put them in one end of the pantry. Eventually, they had taken over virtually all the available space. One night I was looking for a snack and totally unsuspecting, I opened the door to the pantry. All the plastic packaging came tumbling out, raining down on me like a waterfall. When the last bread wrapper fluttered to the floor, I was left standing waist high in Rennee's wrapper collection.

"You never know when you might need it," was all Rennee could say.

The boys and I laughed until we were weak, and soon Rennee was laughing with us. It was clear that love was beginning to grow in our home.

Rennee's exterior transformation had been dramatic and quickly accomplished. Her inner transformation would take considerably longer. She was emotionally damaged and deeply scarred by her life's experiences, and her low self-esteem bordered on self-hatred. She felt clean on the outside, but I believe she doubted that she would feel really clean on the inside ever again. I watched her struggle by herself for a while, but finally I could no longer stand by and say nothing.

"Rennee, do you believe in God?" I asked her one day.

"I used to," Rennee replied honestly. "I even went to church for a while."

"Well, you're welcome to come to church with us any-time," I said.

Later that day I put a copy of the *New Living Bible* on Rennee's nightstand and left it open to the book of John, knowing that this would be an excellent place for Rennee to start her journey towards salvation. Then I left the room and left it up to God.

It wasn't long afterward that Rennee started asking questions, and I knew that God was working in her life. I answered her questions as she asked them, showing her the scriptures in the Bible I had given her. I never pushed her because I knew that God was doing the task, and I was just His assistant.

She used to ask me to tell her stories from the Bible, and it was my pleasure to introduce her to Joseph and Moses and Abraham. But one day she came to me rather troubled.

"How can God love me and forgive me after all I've done?" she asked.

"He forgave David," I told her. "And David sinned grave-ly." I told her how David had desired Bathsheba, the wife of another man, and how David even went so far as to have Bathsheba's husband killed so that he could have her as his wife. "Still, when David cried out to God in true repentance, God forgave him," I explained, as I concluded the story.

"But I've been a prostitute and my past is so full of sin...."

"Your past is not what concerns God, Rennee. If you ask His forgiveness, and make a conscious decision to change the direction of your life, He won't even remember your past. The Bible tells us that He will remove our sins as far as the East is from the West. Do you realize what that means, Rennee? The East will never meet the West.

149

In fact I've just come to understand this myself. We could walk, drive or fly eastward forever and we would never connect with the West. A sin that we confess and repent from ever doing again takes a one-way trip away from us and can never get back."

"So you're saying He could really forgive me...that He could forgive all that I've done?"

"*He* says He will, Rennee. It's not because I say so. God says He will in the Bible I gave you. That verse about removing it as far as the East is from the West is in Psalms 103:12. It says, "As far as the east is from the west, so far hath he removed our transgressions from us." Look for yourself. He is a God of mercy. Remember the story of David that I just told you. He *wants* to forgive. All you need to do is ask."

Eventually, Rennee accepted Christ as her Savior. In fact when she found out that Joseph and I were being baptized, she decided that she would like to be baptized at the same time. I suggested that she wear a sweat suit, not thinking about the fact that a sweat suit would just cling to her body once it got wet. That didn't bother Rennee. She came up out of that water and stood front and center at the church. With the innocence of a child she proclaimed her joy to the whole congregation

"Praise the Lord, I am saved!" she shouted and although there was laughter at her appearance, God's people understood.

Rennee stayed with us until I decided to remarry a man named Colby Cage. At that point, Rennee said she was afraid of my new fiancé, and that she was going to leave. She decided to move back to Chicago. I have often wondered how she is, as I have not seen or heard from her since. Of one thing I am certain. Rennee gave her life to the Lord before she left, and He doesn't begin a work that He doesn't take to completion.

# Chapter
# 19

# The Grand Ball

The invitation came in the mail. I had been invited to a Grand Ball. It had an early 1900s theme; so of course, I was wearing an exquisite ballgown, as were all the other ladies who attended. I was going to meet a prince, and I was ever so excited.

When I arrived at the address on the invitation, it was a huge high-rise hotel with a spacious entrance foyer with large marble columns and sparkling chandeliers. Right in the center was a beautiful winding staircase. All the ballrooms were occupied and I felt very confused. *How will I find the Grand Ball I'm supposed to attend?* I wondered. There are so many rooms, and there seemed to be no one available to ask. There was a large set of double doors on the ground floor and I could hear music, so I decided to try that first.

As I pushed open one of the doors and entered the room, it looked like any other ball I had ever seen. People were dancing and the music was loud. A man in a black tuxedo suddenly walked up to me took my hand and kissed it. *This must be the prince,* I thought, as I followed his lead through the crowd to the edge of the dance floor. I was trembling with excitement and hoping he would ask me to dance. Just as he turned towards me and I prepared myself to accept his invitation, a very pretty blonde lady came up to him. He immediately turned his back to me and they took off across the dance floor, dancing and laughing together.

A voice behind me said, "That is deception."

*Well, if I've been deceived, then I'm getting out of here,* I thought, as I ran from the room.

Finding myself back in the foyer, my gaze lifted to the winding staircase. Two ladies were walking down the stairs together. One lady had skin like polished ebony and was dressed all in silver. Even her hair was adorned with a silver ornament. The other lady had a porcelain complexion and was dressed all in gold. A gold ornament adorned her hair, as well. As they approached me, I was aware that they were even more beautiful than they seemed at a distance. They spoke to me in unison.

"We've come to take you to the Grand Ball. Come with us."

I took my place between them and we seemed to almost float up that spiral staircase. There was a ball-room at the very top. They pushed the doors open for me to enter. The light in that room was so bright I could not see the other people. There was no loud music here, but I found an incomprehensible joy filling my heart. Out of the light came a voice.

"You have made it to the Grand Ball, and this night I will give you your new name. It shall be Diligence."

My dream was over.

When I awoke the next morning, I was so excited about this dream. I rushed to the dictionary to see what diligence meant. I had never used the word but I had heard it. I wanted to know everything about it. Isn't that just the way we all are, though? I wanted to know about the good stuff. I wanted to know about myself and my new name that I felt the Lord had given me. In my haste, I was about to trip over the important part that could keep me from getting there. Deception.

It took me several weeks, perhaps months, to see deception was standing in the way of my wonderful new name. But I know that I am not alone. How do you stop deception in these last days of hectic schedules? Deception has never been easy to spot and in today's world, it can be especially difficult. Satan is the father of lies and deception is a lie. He has been honing his craft for thousands of years, and he knows all the tricks. But he also knows that the game is about to be over, and he will not be allowed to deceive us any more, so he is giving it his best shot in the last minutes of the last quarter. Over thousands of years, he has shaped our belief systems with his deception. We are deceived in so many ways that we begin to take deception for granted. We accept lies as truth and live in the darkness of deceit.

Let me give you an example of what deception is. We have come to believe that one parent can't make enough money for the home to function properly so the mother leaves the home to work. Gradually, ever so gradually, family after family finds itself with both parents in the workplace. Satan employed diversionary tactics over this same period of time to keep us from seeing his deceptive plan. Women began fighting for equal salaries and equal rights to advancement in their jobs. Prayer was taken out of the schools by a Congress that still prays before every session. Double standards were in abundance and they took our focus off Satan's big lie.

Now where is the deception? Today we see a lot of broken homes. Mothers are leaving the home and going to work, and children are being deprived of the stability that her presence in the home previously gave them. Their self-esteem can suffer. Infidelity has become rampant and divorce is commonplace. Some fathers don't even pay child support, much less alimony. The result is that one parent is raising the children on one salary, which Satan just spent years convincing us was impossible when only the father was the breadwinner.

Satan has taught us to believe that it takes a double income to raise a family but day after day single mothers are proving that is not true. They are doing it...and they are doing it on one salary. So what lie have we been sold, and what have we bought into? Deception is so very often tied to our pride and ego. It is no wonder that the Bible is full of Scriptures about pride, such as Proverbs 16:18: "Pride goes before destruction, a haughty spirit before a fall." (NIV)

The deception the Lord wanted me to see in the Grand Ball dream was about the marriage that I was about to enter. It was a marriage that eventually ended with my husband dancing off with a blonde friend of mine, but it would be years before I could see the real meaning this dream had held for me. I did plenty wrong in this marriage and I understand that. I truly believe it takes two to make a marriage and two to break one up. But the Lord knew that I would never try to go back to a man who went after one of my friends. Where that man is concerned, I was iced over in a coldness that would never return to warmth. There did come a time, however, that I did forgive him and also asked for his forgiveness.

I pray this book will open your eyes to deception in its many forms, and that the Lord would sow diligence into your heart as He has mine.

# Chapter
## 20

# Ride In The Rain

Things hadn't been going too well between my new husband, Colby Cage, and me when my son, Joseph, insisted on flying up from Atlanta to visit. I was living in Baltimore by that time, and I knew he wanted me to move to Atlanta. But I wasn't convinced that this was the best course of action for me, so I declined his offer. Still, Joseph was always able to lift my spirits and this visit was no exception. All too soon it was time for him to leave.

The day Joe was to fly home dawned clear and bright, and I prepared to take him to the airport to meet his plane. Since it was such a beautiful, sunny day, we decided to leave the convertible's hard top in the garage and enjoy the warm weather. Besides, I loved the feeling of freedom I got from driving the convertible with its top off.

It was about a forty-five-minute drive to the airport, but it just gave me that much more time with Joseph. As we emerged from the Baltimore Tunnel, we could see the airport up ahead, and surprisingly the sky behind the airport looked black and ominous.

"Wow, Mom!" Joseph exclaimed. "It looks like a pretty nasty storm brewing there. Why don't you just drop me off at the terminal and start right back. You can probably outrun it if you don't go in with me."

I hesitated. I wanted to give Joseph a proper good-bye, but looking at the sky, I felt he was probably right. I just might be able to get back ahead of it if I hurried. Besides, I'd left the convertible's top in the garage; so unless I could stay ahead of the storm, I was about to get very wet.

I pulled up to the terminal and Joseph bounded out of the car. Grabbing his luggage from the back, he raced around to the driver's side and planted a good-bye kiss on my cheek.

"I love you, Mother. Drive safely. I'll let you know when I get back home. By the way, Mom, you can always pull under an overpass if it starts to rain. Drivers do that all the time."

"I love you, too, Joseph," I called out to him. "And I'll remember about the overpass," I added, as I swung the convertible around and headed back home.

As I pulled out onto the main highway, it was clear that hurrying was not going to be as easy as I had thought. The traffic was bumper to bumper in the tunnel. As I inched along, I became more and more nervous. Being stuck in traffic that is barely moving always makes me somewhat anxious, but now that I was stuck inside this tunnel and trying to outrun a thunderstorm, it was almost more than I could take. I felt my chest tighten with the familiar anxiety of not being able to control the situation.

Finally, the traffic flow eased as I drove out of the tunnel. The road became four lanes and I was able to pick up speed. I was even pushing the steering wheel as well as the accelerator as if that would help me go faster. Maybe, just maybe, I could still get home in time. No sooner had that thought come into my mind than large drops of rain began to hit the windshield. Very quickly the rain began to come down in blinding sheets and even with the windshield wipers on high, it was very hard to see. I spotted an overpass just ahead, and I remembered Joseph's suggestion. *I could pull under until the storm passed,* I thought. I was seriously considering this option when I was startled by a voice.

**"LOOK AT YOURSELF. ARE YOU WET?"**

Automatically, I looked down at myself for the first time. I was wearing a deep purple silk blouse and there was not a spot on it.

"No," I responded out loud, totally surprised that I wasn't drenched.

**"I'M GOING TO TAKE CARE OF YOU,"** the voice continued.

Even so, I hesitated, braking ever so slightly as a second overpass came into sight up ahead. I could still take shelter there until the storm passed. There was still time to pull over.

**"LOOK AT YOURSELF,"** the voice instructed me again. **"ARE YOU WET?"** it asked.

Again I glanced down in amazement at the still-dry silk blouse and once again the voice reassured me.

**"I'M GOING TO TAKE CARE OF YOU."**

"Okay, Lord," I said, now quite sure of the source of the voice. "I know I should be soaked by now but I'm not, so I am going to go on, just trusting You."

By this time, I had just gone under a third overpass and the rain was still falling in torrents. I could see it soaking the ground, the trees and creating puddles here and there. The rain came down like a solid sheet of water in front of me and beside me. It was then that I thought of Peter. I believe I know how he felt that night when he began walking on the water toward Jesus in the midst of the storm. As I glanced in my rearview mirror, there was a similar sheet of rain behind me. I turned the wipers on high and still had nearly zero visibility. Again the voice asked the same question.

**"LOOK AT YOURSELF. ARE YOU WET?"**

Looking down at myself, I was amazed to realize that despite the storm swirling all around me, I was still completely dry.

"No, Lord," I admitted aloud. "I'm not wet at all and I won't look at the storm any more. Let's just enjoy this ride together."

**"I'M GOING TO TAKE CARE OF YOU,"** the voice assured me again and then it was silent.

A van passed me. In the back seat, children were jumping up and down, shouting to their parents excitedly and pointing. They were pointing at the lady who was driving her convertible in the midst of a terrible deluge, but who wasn't even getting wet. They were pointing at me!

I was about two miles from my home when all the rain stopped. I pulled into the driveway. I jumped out of the car and ran in the house to get Colby. I had noticed that his sleek convertible was in the driveway with its top down.

"Colby, come quick," I called out to him from the front door. "You need to put the top up on your car while I go get the top to mine out of the garage. I've just been driving in a torrential rain storm and it will be here any minute."

"Toni," Colby replied. "What are you talking about? There's not a cloud in the sky."

"There's a storm coming. I promise you. I just drove through it. You really should put the top up on your car."

"Nonsense," Colby snorted, as he walked out to the cars. "There's not a drop of water on you and the inside of your car is dry as a bone. You'd be soaked if you had driven with the top down through even a small rainstorm. But look at you. Your clothes are completely dry, and you don't even have a hair out of place. You can't convince me there's any rain coming."

Realizing that Colby was not going to listen, I ran to the garage and got the top for my car and began fastening it on the car.

"Please, Colby. It *will* rain and you *will* want to have the top up on your car," I warned him one more time.

"Forget it, Toni," he said. "IT'S NOT GOING TO RAIN!"

He had barely finished speaking when the first drops of rain hit his face. Before Colby had time to turn around, much less get the top up on his convertible, the bottom fell out and rain poured from the sky like a dam had been opened. Colby's jaw dropped in total amazement. He ran for his car and did get the top up, but not before his car was good and flooded inside. We ran for the house, but by the time we made it to the porch, we were both soaked and looked like a couple of drowned rats. We stood there in silence, just watching it rain, for quite some time. Finally Colby spoke.

"There is no way that you drove for an hour in rain like that with no top on your car without getting wet," Colby fumed. "I don't believe you."

"You never want to believe anything the Lord does for me, Colby. And you know what? It really doesn't matter whether you believe me or not anymore. The important thing is what *I* know and I know that I know. My God is awesome and He loves me. He would show His love for you, too, if you would only let Him."

# Chapter
## 21

# *Three Miracles*

*I* had not been married to Colby even six months and I knew it was over, but I had really known that on the honeymoon. When you spend three hours of your wedding night watching your new husband give all of his attention to your beautiful friend, you know something is very wrong with this picture. But that is exactly what Colby did.

My friend, Peg, had given me my wedding dress and prepared a small reception at her home with cake and champagne before we were to leave for our honeymoon. Colby took full advantage of the situation as he sat on a barstool with his back to me and flirted with Peg. Finally, we left her house to go to our honeymoon suite, and I felt sure that I would now have Colby's complete attention. I was wrong. Colby insisted I call Peg so we could take her to breakfast the next morning. This is too much and I decided to put my foot down.

"Colby Cage, this is *our* honeymoon. I don't intend to share you with anyone."

I expected him to apologize and see things my way, but instead I was knocked to the floor by the man I'd just married. Others had seen my marrying Colby as a mistake, but I had not listened. The pastor at my church had counseled against this marriage, and had actually refused to marry us. When my friend Joanna first met

Colby, she had taken me aside, and tried to warn me as well.

"The Lord showed me this man has two sets of eyes. One was a set of snake eyes. He will take you away from your home and friends, and he's going to hurt you. Please hear me," she pleaded.

Sitting there on the floor of my honeymoon suite, I suddenly remembered a dream I had been given from the Lord on the night before my wedding. It had been my third warning–my third confirmation–and I had ignored them all.

In the dream, Colby said he had a surprise for me. We were in his car and he drove us to an airport. A plane was waiting there, but it was no fancy jet or modern plane. It looked like an old World War I two-seater airplane. A pilot sat in the cockpit. He had on one of those tight leather caps and a leather jacket. As we approached the plane, I was protesting furiously.

"Please. I don't want to do this. You know I'm afraid of flying. Being closed in where I can't get out reminds me of the attic. Please don't ask me to do this. It will be torture, Colby. Surprises are supposed to be fun and this will be far from fun for me."

"Calm down," he told me. "I have plans to get you over your fear. You'll see. This will be a big step for you and I'll be with you all the way. Trust me. This will be the adventure of a lifetime. Now hush whining and come on," He insisted.

Reluctantly, I followed Colby to the plane. When I crawled into the seat behind the pilot, I saw that Colby was already sitting in the only space there was.

"I have no place to sit," I said.

"Yes, you do. Right here in my lap where you will be safe. Just straddle my legs and face me."

At the same time I sat on his lap, he was buckling the safety belt around his waist, but there was no safety belt to buckle around me.

"I can't do this," I began to protest again. He tightened his grip around my waist with his arms, and he began to promise me how he would hold on to me and not let go.

"What if the pilot does loops? Then I will fall out for sure," I said.

"Well, he isn't going to do any loops, so you just settle in for a nice ride."

The plane began to taxi down the runway; and as soon as he left the ground, the pilot immediately went into a big loop. I was screaming at the top off my lungs.

"I'm falling. You lied. I'm not safe. Make him stop, Colby. I'm falling. I'm not secure."

I woke up, my body damp with sweat. But I had not heeded the dream's warning. I had dismissed it as just a nightmare, probably stemming from something I had eaten. Three times God had tried to speak to me. He tried through my pastor. He tried through my friend, and He tried through my dream. I had closed my eyes and ears and married Colby anyway.

Now, here I was six months later. I was married to Colby and was solely dependent upon him. I had no job, no money of my own, and a car that cost $250 a month. I still had Bryan in high school, and I received no child support from his biological father. I felt I should leave this marriage, but how was I going to get free?

I was sitting on my couch, praying, when the doorbell rang. As I opened my door, to my surprise, there stood one of the prayer warriors from the little church I was attending.

"The Lord sent me here to tell you He is going to take care of you," she said.

I was stunned. She had just used the same words I had heard the voice say to me when I rode in the convertible in the rain. I had not discussed my situation with her and there was no way that she could have known I had any problems. I had been so careful to make sure that everyone at church saw me as happy in my marriage. How could this woman have known?

"Thank you," I said, unable to think of any other response at the time. "Would you like to come in?" I thought that if she came in I might be able to better understand why she had said what she did

"No," she replied. "I'm on my way to work, but I felt I must tell you now."

"Thank you again," I said, still somewhat confused by the encounter. We gave each other a friendly hug and she was gone. I went to my living room, sat on the couch, and pondered what she had said.

"How can You take care of me, Lord? I'm in such a mess and I haven't listened to Your warnings."

"Just take a step and I will show you."

"One step? Okay, Lord. I can do that." I called another of the prayer warriors of the church I attended. She was a bank teller, and I asked if she would meet me during her lunch hour and pray with me. She quickly agreed, adding that another lady from the prayer team would be there also. She told me to meet her at the bank and we would be able to use a conference room there.

I arrived promptly at twelve-thirty, and told them my situation. By now I had decided that I needed to leave

164

immediately. Colby was planning to be in Chicago on business, and that would give me three days to move out while he was gone. I requested that they pray with me that I would find a job. At that particular time, I wasn't really concerned about where I would go or where I would live. My first priority was to get a job to provide the income I would need to support my child and pay my car payment.

I shared with them that I knew of a company that had an opening. It was a company that was in competition with my husband's business, and I felt I could do the job. Although I honestly didn't think they would consider me, I wanted to try. We began to pray in agreement.

As we continued to pray, the other two women seemed convinced that I was to go for this particular job. I made a phone call and requested an interview. Within one hour, I was in the president's office. This company was based in Baltimore, Maryland, and at that time had no accounts in North Carolina or even near there. But I wanted to go home and I promised the company president that I could and I would build a territory there. To my amazement, he accepted my proposal and I was hired. With the interview over, we began to walk towards the door when the president asked me to wait a moment while he went back in his office. When he came out, he laid a thousand dollar check in my hand. I looked in astonishment.

"What is this for? I haven't even worked a day for you yet."

"It's so you'll have a safe move. I trust you."

This was a miracle. What I was yet to discover was it was only the first miracle. Within twenty-four hours of meeting with the prayer group, God had two more miracles planned for me.

I went straight home from my job interview and began calling movers, trying to make some arrangements before my husband came home at six. He would not be leaving for Chicago until the next morning. I made call after call and there was not one moving company that could take me on such short notice. They were all booked. I even tried U-Haul® and they were booked. *Oh my,* I thought. *This is not good. What am I going to do?*

Suddenly I thought of a friend I had in North Carolina. She was a very bright, creative lady and she seemed to have the ability to work almost anything out. I quickly dialed her number, hoping to get some ideas. She knew that I was in an abusive relationship, as I had visited her while my arm was in a cast from falling down a flight of stairs after being hit by my husband. So I knew she would be more than willing to help me.

"Hi Peg," I began. "It's Toni. I need your help. I'm leaving Colby. I have a job but I can't find a mover."

"Just sit by your phone. I'll fix it," she said and the phone went dead. I hung up the receiver on my end. It was only fifteen minutes before the phone rang.

"Good afternoon, young lady. This is Rick Eastman of Eastman Brothers Movers out of Raleigh. Your friend Peg said you were in a little trouble up there."

"Yes, I am. Can you help me?"

"We've just dispatched a truck. It's on its way to get you, so get ready."

"Thank you so much. I'll be ready."

There it was. Miracle Number Two. But I didn't really realize this at the time.

Oh my goodness! It hit me. I had put the cart before the horse. Where was I moving? I didn't have any place to move my furniture to. The movers are now on their way, and I don't even know where to tell them to take my belongings. How will I ever find a place and be ready when they arrive?

Another friend's name was impressed on my mind. She is a very resourceful lady, so I planned to call her first thing the next morning.

That night, Colby was busy preparing for his trip and I went to bed early to stay out of his way. As soon as he was gone the next morning, I called Mary Lou. It was early in the day, but I knew she was an early riser. I didn't have to go into detail because she also knew how Colby had abused me. In fact she had stayed with me when my arm had been in a brace from one of his rampages, and she had witnessed first-hand the tension in our home.

"Mary Lou, I need your help," I said. "I have a job and the movers will be here tomorrow, but I don't have an apartment. I can send you some money for gas. Would you drive to Raleigh and see if you could find an apartment for me? I'll pay you as soon as I get there."

"I haven't got a dime to put a deposit down or gas money so I really can't get to Raleigh," she replied. "But, the Lord just impressed on me that you're not to go to Raleigh. You're to go to Greensboro."

"Greensboro? You're crazy. I've never been to that city and I don't know anyone there. At least I have friends in Raleigh."

"Nope. It's Greensboro. I'll call you after I've checked out a few places. Let me go. I've got to get dressed."

"Okay. Call me as soon as you know anything."

It was close to twelve when Mary Lou called back.

"Well," she began. "I have the keys in my hand to a beautiful, sun-filled, peach-carpeted, overlooking-the-pool apartment. You will love it! Also, it is only a few blocks from the best church in Greensboro. You'll love going to the Cathedral of His Glory.

"You're kidding! You have the key! Where did you get the money for the deposit?"

"I didn't give her one. You can do that when you get here."

"And she gave you the key with no money down? No lease signed or anything? You sure are a good talker."

"It's not just talking when the Lord is on your side," she said.

"Well, I can't thank you enough even though I don't really want to go to Nineveh...I mean, Greensboro."

Miracle Number Three. I looked at the clock. It was twelve-thirty. In just twenty-four hours I had received all three miracles. God had definitely kept His promise to take care of me.

# Chapter
## 22

# *The Lord Came To See My New House*

After seven months of separation, Colby and I reconciled. Once again, he convinced me he had changed. He even quit his job in Maryland and moved to North Carolina and into the apartment the Lord had provided for my escape from him just seven months before. The spellbinding spirit of abuse had captured me again and the cycle started all over. I was strangely drawn to this pattern of his talking down to me, followed by "the silent treatment," followed by presents that he gave me in a lavish attempt to make up for his bad behavior. But this time I was discovering new ways to cope. I would get sick and the doctors would prescribe plenty of drugs for my pain. I found that adding alcohol to the mixture further dulled the reality of my situation.

House hunting can be an exhausting and frustrating task, but not this time. Even though Colby had found a job in Greensboro, we decided to look for a house in another town where we could get a nicer home at a more reasonable rate. I had informed the realtor that I wanted a lot of light, and that a big kitchen where my family could gather was essential. I love to cook, and I knew that if I were to spend time with my family as well, they would have to come into the kitchen.

I never suspected that she would find the perfect house immediately. but as it turned out, the first house we looked at was the only one. I fell in love with its spaciousness and its abundance of windows. It was nestled in the woods with no homes nearby. There were other homes a distance up the road, but it was very private. My husband, Colby, loved it as well, and we both agreed that it was just what we wanted, so we signed the papers that day. Within a couple of weeks, we were all settled in. On the surface, it appeared that we had everything going for us. My husband had his new job, we had our new home, which allowed us to live near my friends, and money was certainly no problem. Yes, everything around us seemed so perfect–yet here I was...crying myself to sleep.

I didn't have the answers but I certainly did have a lot of questions. I remember thinking *I just don't understand, Lord. Colby and I fight like two wild animals. I really can't take much more. This marriage is more illusion than reality. It has all the outward appearance of the perfect marriage, a beautiful home and clothes, a luxurious lifestyle, but the inner workings of this marriage are all haywire. Please help me, Father. I want to die. Take me home with You. I can't be a good mother or a good wife. I just don't know how. I try. You know how hard I try. But I try and I fail. That failure is slowly killing me. I really mean it, Lord. I want to die.* My desperate thoughts continued to plague me, and when sleep finally overtook me that night, I had a very unusual dream. The Lord had come to see my new house.

I was so excited when I opened the front door and realized who was there. I didn't see a face or a body in the dream. It was more a feeling of a presence standing there, but there was no doubt in my mind who that presence was.

"Oh, Lord, You've come to see my new house. I'm so glad. Please come in."

We walked through the foyer into the living room and I slid open the door to the deck.

"I would like to show you the backyard first," I told Him as we walked out onto the spacious deck. I walked up to the rail of the deck, anxious to have Him see the beauty of the land behind my house. As I turned to point out the tall pines that lined the edges of the property, something very strange happened. Instead of looking out across the flat, manicured grass to the trees, I found myself looking into a deep canyon...only this canyon had no bottom. It was like the abyss spoken of in the Book of Revelation.

I drew back from the rail quickly and said, "Oh, Lord. We are in the wrong house. My backyard is flat. This is not my house."

**"THIS IS YOUR HOUSE,"** the presence spoke for the first time.

"It can't be," I responded. "Let's go inside so I can see my furniture. I really think we are in the wrong neighborhood."

We stepped back inside the house and I scanned the living room. All the furnishings were in their proper places and they were all mine. But as I looked upward, something very unusual caught my eye. A huge boulder was coming right through the ceiling.

"Lord," I protested again. "We really are in the wrong house. My house does not have any boulders jutting through the ceiling."

**"THIS IS YOUR HOUSE,"** the presence spoke again.

Stubborn and rebellious as ever, I just would not accept that this was my house.

"Lord, would you mind if we walked out into the front yard so I can stand back and get a good perspective of this house?" There was no answer so I proceeded to walk out the front door and out into the middle of the front yard. As I turned around to get a good look at the house, I gasped. There was an *entire mountain* sitting on top of my house! The house appeared to have been built into a crevice, and it was clear that the entire weight of the mountain rested on it.

"Lord, this proves it," I declared. "This is obviously not my house. There are not any mountains in the area where we live."

### "THIS IS YOUR HOUSE."

Now He had told me the same thing three times and quite frankly, I was getting a little perturbed. I knew where I lived and this was NOT it!

Still unconvinced, I walked with the presence back into the house. Again I found myself in a room that certainly resembled my living room. Suddenly everything in the house began to tremble. An earthquake! I grabbed the back of my sofa for something to hold on to and as everything began to sway, I woke up, grasping my bed-covers tightly in both hands.

I lay there for a minute, gradually becoming aware that I have been dreaming. Then I got up and went into the living room. I sat down on the sofa and began to go back over the dream in my mind.

"I know this dream was from You, Lord," I admitted. "And I think You are telling me that there is a mountain on my marriage. I am just depending upon You to show me what that mountain is."

Had I stopped there, I probably would have been given my answer very quickly, but I sometimes think I am so smart that I have to tell God what He is trying to tell me. Talking instead of listening can be a stumbling block. Still, it was a beautiful lesson He was about to teach me.

For three months this was my prayer. "Father, God. I just know that my marital problems stem from my husband's unfaithfulness and I know the mountain on our marriage is his affair. So please, Father, expose him and show me where this woman lives."

Now I'm sure you'll agree that was a great prayer. Didn't I have it all figured out?

The problem was that my husband was home every night and never went anywhere. I don't know when I thought he could be having this affair, but I knew the problem had to be another woman because he surely seemed to dislike me a lot.

After three months of not hearing an answer, I finally reworded my prayer.

"Lord, I know this dream was from You and I can't figure it out. If the mountain on my marriage isn't Colby having an affair, then is it something I'm doing?"

The answer was immediate. "I would not give you a dream to clean up Colby Cage!"

"Well, that was a profound statement, Lord, and it makes a lot of sense. I just don't understand what in the world you could want to clean up in me that's as big as a mountain."

Suddenly a thought hit me that made me start to cry. "Oh, Lord, are you going to break up my marriage? Is that what the earthquake meant?"

Instantly the earthquake scene flashed before my eyes again. This time, as I stood there holding onto the sofa, I looked all around the room. I had lots of crystal angels and vases, but nothing was broken.

"If you are not going to break up my marriage, are you going to shake up my marriage?" I ventured. "Whatever it is, Father, that You want me to do, I humbly come to You and yield myself. Clean me up. Whatever it is, show me, Father." With my brief prayer finished, I went to bed.

When the right prayer is prayed, an answer comes. That is for sure. From that day forward, I began to stand on Matthew 7:7. "Ask, and it shall be given you; seek, and you shall find; knock, and it shall be opened unto you." (KJV)

The next morning I was awakened by the telephone ringing.

"Hi, Toni. This is Becky York. I'm in Greensboro today and quite frankly, I don't know what I'm doing here. I flew in yesterday to visit my daughter but she's quite busy, and I really feel like I'm just in the way. I'd love to see you while I'm here. Why don't you call Jody, and perhaps both of you could come over tonight." Becky was a long-time friend from back in my "hippie days", long before this marriage.

"Great," I said. "I'll call her right now!"

Jody was free that night and we both were excited to get a chance to spend an evening with Becky. We arrived at Becky's daughter's house, and after a while Becky began to share her AA (Alcoholics Anonymous) story with us. She wanted us both to know how great it was to be sober. Usually I would have tuned out on this type of discussion, but for some reason, I began to listen with new ears. It just seemed as if the things she said she now had—like peace and joy—were the very things I wanted. She talked about the treatment center she had gone to and about how much love she received there.

*I sure could stand some of that*, I thought.

All too soon, it was time to leave. Jody and I had come in separate cars, so we all said our good-byes and I headed for mine. I was barely inside the car when I began to cry. Something just seemed to be breaking up inside me. My drive home became another confrontation with the Lord.

"Okay, Lord. Is this it? Is my drinking the mountain on my marriage? Do you think I'm an alcoholic? Well, I just find that hard to believe, Lord. I don't think I *act* like an alcoholic. I don't go stumbling around places drunk. I have never gotten a DWI, or had to be taken home or any of those things alcoholics do. But this has to be what You're showing me, though. At this point, I don't know of anything else that it could be. Should I check out a treatment center?" The Lord left me to ponder my own questions.

When I walked through the door, Colby could tell I had been crying.

"What's wrong?" he asked.

"I've decided to go to a treatment center for alcoholics. Will you help me find one?"

Now we were both crying, and Colby wanted to know what had made me decide to do this. I told him about my evening and about Becky's story. I capped my explanation off with this statement: "Well, if everyone in this family thinks I have a drinking problem, then I want to go and do something about it." Did you notice how I said if *everyone*...thinks? I didn't actually believe that I was an alcoholic. I wanted to go to the treatment center because I intended to prove to God and everyone else that I *wasn't* an alcoholic. Tucked away in the back of my

175

mind, like a gambler's ace in the hole, was the belief that I could go to the treatment center and prove that I was only a social drinker, and that the professional staff there would back me up.

Colby was more than agreeable and was able to quickly work out the details...perhaps a little too quickly, I thought. He assured me that Fellowship Hall was an excellent facility and I had agreed to go. But the day before I was to actually be admitted to the program there, I told Colby that I didn't want him to take me to the center. I didn't explain to him why I felt this way, but it was a combination of my being embarrassed, and my now blaming Colby for my actually having to follow through with this. Since this was my last "free" day, I told my friend, Jody, that I wanted to go to a bar and have one of every drink I might ever want again. Needless to say, I didn't feel very great the next day when I was sitting in the admittance office at Fellowship Hall.

After all the forms had been signed and the rules had been explained to me, a staff member showed me to my room. As I entered the room, I glanced at the number on the door. It was the number six. I knew that six was the number that the Bible uses to represent flesh, and I was keenly aware of the fact that it was a problem with the flesh and my old nature that had put me in this room. After the attendant left, I sat on my bed wondering how in the world I ever got to this place in my life. I felt as if I was getting ready to have a scarlet letter "A" branded on my chest–alcoholic for the rest of my life.

The next week flew by. They had us doing so much stuff that it was impossible to be bored. Both the classes and the films were informative–and in the group sessions, I was hearing some very familiar stories. While I was there, I made a new friend. Judy lived across the hall. This was her second time at Fellowship Hall and she was worried that she would not make it.

176

"Oh, you'll make it this time," I told her. "Look what room you're in. It's seven and seven is the Biblical number for completion."

If only I could have felt so sure about my own progress. By the end of the first week, I found myself on my knees beside my bed.

"Father," I prayed. "I'm sorry for the attitude that I came in here with. But I honestly did not believe that I was an alcoholic. I know after this week of education on the subject that I truly am an alcoholic. Most of all, Lord, I realize that I can't get sober and clean up my life by myself. So this day I lay myself on the altar, and I humbly ask for Your help. Mold me and make me into what You want me to be. Strengthen me and give me Your peace."

As I completed my prayer, I found my body racked with sobs as I finally let go of all my pent-up emotion. My tears had just begun to subside when there was a knock on the door. I got up, wiping tears from my face, and opened the door. It was the floor nurse.

"I've come to tell you that we are moving you," she explained. "Please get your things together. You will be moving into room seven."

I closed the door and fell back on my knees. Now I was *really sobbing*. "Thank you, Father, for telling me that You will take me to completion by placing me in room seven."

The weeks that followed were now an exciting adventure for me. I was finding out things that I had hidden in the back corners of my mind. I was beginning to see how these closed off places that I had inside me were impacting my feelings about life. Let me give you an example. The first two weeks I was at Fellowship Hall, I was not allowed to have any visitors. This was true for everyone in the program. So, the first visit from my husband was very traumatic. A part of me really missed my family, but another part of me was like a freshly plowed field. All that "stuff" underneath that I had buried so deeply had been turned over and now lay on the top side. I wondered what would happen if he saw it and then didn't like me because of it. I didn't know who the real me was yet and I felt very vulnerable. I found that being vulnerable is a necessary part of getting well.

Visitation started at six p.m. and lasted only one hour. At seven p.m., a film was scheduled. The first night I could have visitors, I found a chair right in front of a window that overlooked the entrance gate. I sat watching, my heart jumping with each car that entered. But as the minutes ticked by, there was still no Colby and no Bryan, my son. All too soon, it was 7:00 p.m. and we were being called in to view the film. I went in quickly so I could save two seats on the front row for my husband and my son. It seemed as if everyone wanted those two seats, and with each person's attempt to claim them, I was getting madder and madder. How dare they embarrass me like this! I can't adequately describe the feelings I was having.

When the film was over, I walked out into the lobby only to see Colby playing pool at one of the pool tables. I was furious...so furious that I couldn't even talk with him beyond choking out, "You might as well go home. I'm certainly not visiting with you."

I turned and ran sobbing down the hall to my room and slammed the door. Colby was right behind me, but when he opened the door, I wouldn't even let him talk. I was trembling all over and was screaming.

"Get out of here. You are not allowed in my room. I told you. I'm not visiting. Go!"

"Didn't you notice that Bryan is not with me?" he asked, managing to interrupt me briefly. "I'm late because I waited for him, and he didn't show up."

"I don't care what your excuse is," I told him. "Go home."

The feelings I had were so overpowering that I couldn't come out of my anger, not even with a perfectly legitimate excuse. I couldn't and I wouldn't forgive it. Understanding that he could not reason with me at this point, Colby left. After the door closed, I laid on my bed crying for a long time before I decided to talk with God.

"Father," I began. "They are teaching us in here that when we come to a place that we don't understand, that we should ask You the question and You will help us understand. Well, I'm asking. I feel a hurt that is indescribable. It overpowers me. Now that I am talking to You about it, I realize that this pain happens a lot. It seems to come up when people are late and I wonder why that was so. I remember the many fights that Colby and I had had when he would be just five or ten minutes late from work. I feel he should have called to tell me that he would be late but he didn't. Then by the time he did get home, I was a raving banshee.

"Father, I know this isn't right. But I don't know what it is that comes over me and makes me be so out of control. Please help me. I don't want to hurt my family."

The Lord is so wonderful when your heart is humble. Right before my eyes He began showing me a scene from my childhood. It was the day that I stood waiting for my mother to come and get me, and take me home from the farm and away from the attic. The memory of the long hours I waited by the side of the road, and of my mother's emphatic refusal to take me with her that day was as fresh as if it was happening right there in the treatment center. There "IT" was!

"I can feel it, Lord! And now I know what it is; this feeling that so overpowers me. I know what it is! It's the feeling I had as a five-year-old child, a five-year-old child who was waiting and expecting acceptance, only to be

rejected. Oh, Father, thank You for making me understand where this feeling comes from. Now I don't ever
have to go through that feeling...not ever again."

I will admit that the first few times after that when I
was put in a situation where someone was going to be
late, those old feelings tried to rear their ugly heads
again. But then I remembered the Scripture which says,
"Greater is He that is in you than he that is in the world."
(I John 4:4 - KJV) My Father had allowed me to see into
my past as clearly as if I had been watching a video. I
could see the source of the pain and over time, with His
help, I was able to overcome it. Praise God.

I am truly thankful for the treatment center and the
many things I learned while there. Perhaps most impor-
tantly, my coming home sober with no dulling drugs or
alcohol gave me a new perspective. I was able to see the
situation I had chosen for my children and myself more
clearly. It was then that I began my plan to build a
"Noah's Ark" that would provide my means of escape
from this sick marriage that threatened to drown us all.
I informed Colby that I would be opening a Christian
bookstore, but I knew that I was preparing to build a
boat of financial security that would take me out of the
marriage.

# Chapter
## 23

# The Wreck

---

**"Get up! Go to the living room and pray."**

Eyelids heavy with sleep, I peered at the clock on the bedside table. Two-thirty in the morning. It was not an uncommon time for the Lord to wake me, but on this night, He wanted me to leave my warm bed and go to the living room to pray.

"Please Lord," I pleaded, not wanting to leave my cozy cocoon. "I can pray just as well right here in my warm bed."

**"Go to the living room,"** He demanded again.

Rebellious child that I am, I presented my most convincing arguments to God, hoping to change His mind.

"But Lord, today when I was in the living room, a huge spider came out from under the couch. And You know that I don't find spiders one of Your most lovable creatures. In fact, I can't really think of a spider that I ever have liked. Besides, all the lights are off in the living room and that spider could be anywhere."

I could easily visualize stepping on that big brown spider on my way to turn on a lamp, which was all the way across the room. My fear was growing, and I gave it one last effort to convince God that staying warm and cozy in bed would do just as well.

"Did I mention that the heat was off in the living room, Lord? It's bound to be really cold in there by now..."

**"Go to the living room and pray for Bryan,"** the voice commanded for a third time, its urgency unmistakable.

"Okay, Lord. Three is enough for me. I'm up and on my way."

As I reached the doorway to the living room, I saw that all my fears had been for nothing. Not only had the lights been turned on, but the heat was also on; it was usually off in that end of the house. The room was now softly lit, warm and inviting. I stood in that doorway and wept, knowing that God had prepared the room for just this purpose.

Again came His prompting. It was clear that He wanted me to pray for my son, Bryan. The Lord was not specific about what the problem might be that I should pray about, but there was an overwhelming sense of danger. Danger and my son. I knew this was serious and I began to pray for my son. First, I began to bind any assignment on his life. I pleaded for angels to surround him at this time. I prayed for God to send His angels to guard and protect him. Lastly, I pleaded the blood of Jesus over my son's life and ended in Jesus' name. It wasn't a long prayer, but I had presented my petition to God and I knew there was no more for me to do. I turned off the lights and returned to my bedroom. Peace surrounded me. Bryan was now safely placed in the hands of his Heavenly Father.

This wasn't the first time God had warned me that my son, Bryan, was in danger. I came very close to missing the Lord's warning. It was about three years before this, as I remember. I was given a dream. In the dream, Bryan was fishing. He was standing on a huge smooth round rock and I stood on a rock below him near the water. I raised my head and stood looking up at him. All of a sudden, I was aware that there were huge black snakes coming to the surface of the water. There were so many that they were crawling on top of each other.

Panicked at the site of this crawling, living nest of snakes, I called out to my son, "Bryan! You can't fish here. It's too dangerous!"

"I know what I'm doing," he yelled back. With an air of confidence, he came off the rock and walked past me to a shoreline where a motorboat was waiting. Two water skis were lying on the shore near the boat. To my horror, Bryan put on the skis and picked up the towrope. He motioned to the boat's driver that he was ready, and the boat began to draw my son out into the treacherous waters. On either side of the lake were cement walls, one rising high on Bryan's left and the other rising up equally high on his right. As the boat towed Bryan to the center of the lake, he dropped the rope and went under. Holding my breath, I waited for him to surface. But Bryan didn't come up.

For the first time, I became aware of a dark-haired girl standing beside me. I didn't recognize her, as things happened too quickly for me to get a chance to see her face. I stood frozen in my tracks on the shore. How could I ever reach my son with all those snakes between us? As I stood unable to move, the girl at my side dove in the water. Somehow her action gave me courage and I jumped into the water right behind her. When I finally reached the spot where Bryan had gone under, I felt as if I was looking down into the cavernous mouth of a tornado. I could see Bryan's arm and hand reaching up towards me. I reached down into the whirling water and caught his hand. With all my strength, I pulled my son out of the abyss and to safety.

I had been staying with my friend, Mary Lou, while I was on a business trip and the next morning, I brought up the dream. "Mary Lou, I've had a rather disturbing dream. I really don't know what to make of it. I don't know if it's a warning, or what."

I proceeded to tell my friend about the dream in detail. After I finished, she spoke with authority.

"We need to pray, Toni. We need to bind Satan's assignments against Bryan. We need to pray for his protection."

Mary Lou grasped my hand and with a simple prayer, she bound the assignment, prayed for protection, and placed Bryan in God's care. "You can rest now, Toni. God has given you an opportunity to pray for your child for a reason. We may not know what that reason is, but we do know that God will hear our prayer and protect Bryan."

I believed, as Mary Lou said, that we had done all we could about this, and after two or three days, I had forgotten about even having the dream.

It was a Sunday afternoon. Bryan's birthday had been the day before, and I had given him a new, top-of-the-line casting rod and reel. He was so excited about his new fishing gear he couldn't wait to use it. He asked if I would take him and one of his friends fishing when we got home from church. Of course, I agreed. I was very pleased that he liked my gift so much.

I drove the boys to the local dam, which was a popular fishing spot. I pulled the car to a stop at the top of a hill overlooking a meadow, which led to the dam. I watched as the boys walked down to the meadow, then called out to them as I turned back towards the car.

"I'll be back at five o'clock," I promised.

As I was driving away, a feeling of uneasiness came over me, but I quickly shrugged it off. It was a gorgeous day and things were going well in my life. There was absolutely no reason to feel anything but wonderful, I reasoned.

I had only been home a few minutes when there was a knock on the door. When I opened the door I found one of my girlfriends, Tiann, standing there. She had come by to show me her new Corvette convertible and she was bubbling over with excitement.

"Come for a ride in my new car," she coaxed. "I can't wait to have you share the fun of cruising around in my convertible."

I was excited and pleased for her and usually I wouldn't have hesitated for a second, but this time I did hesitate. The feeling of uneasiness I had felt before had suddenly gripped me even harder.

"I can't," I said. "I have to pick Bryan up at five o'clock. If we get out, you'll be showing your car to everyone and I might be late. Besides," I admitted, "I really feel uneasy about something. I can't explain why but I just know that I have to be there at five o'clock, so I'd better not go with you."

"Oh, please, please go with me," she begged. "I promise I will leave no matter where we are. As a matter of fact, I promise I'll even leave early so we won't be late."

"Are you sure I won't be stranded?" I asked, still not fully convinced I should go.

"I promise," she said with such sincerity that I finally gave in.

"I'm holding you to your word," I cautioned her as I climbed into her car.

The day was perfect for a ride in a convertible, and I soon let myself relax. We had a great time driving around and showing off Tiann's car. At four o'clock, however, Tiann, true to her word, looked at me and said, "Let's go get Bryan."

"Great," I said, pleased that she was being so considerate. But even as we drove towards the dam, that unsettled feeling grabbed me one more time.

Looking back, I should have thought about the dream I had earlier and been more on the alert. But when we pulled up to the top of the hill, I didn't recognize anything from the dream, so I still didn't make any connection. As a matter of fact, I was just sitting there in the car, blowing the horn, hoping the boys would hear it and I wouldn't have to walk all the way down to the dam to get them. I wasn't paying too much attention at that point, so I didn't even notice the young boy running across the field toward our car in an evident panic.

Tiann saw him first and jumped out of the car. Quickly climbing over the fence that surrounded the meadow, she ran to meet him in the field. I saw her bend down and listen as the boy said something in her ear. Then, grabbing her hand, the boy took off running towards the dam, dragging Tiann behind him. Up until this point, I had been immobile, just watching what was happening without really comprehending. But it was just like in my dream.

The girl with the long, dark hair went first in the dream and now Tiann was already on her way to the dam, her long, dark hair blowing in the breeze. As the realization that something was very wrong finally hit me, I jumped out of the car and ran after them as fast as I could. When I got to the dam, I was actually standing on a rock below where Tiann and the boy were holding my son, Bryan. They appeared to be trying to talk him out of something. Fear gripped me and I scrambled up to the large round rock where they were all gathered. When I finally got to them, I felt as if my heart would pound out of my chest.

"What's wrong?" I gasped.

"If you had been one minute later," Bryan's friend said, "I couldn't have stopped him from jumping."

I was stunned. Why in the world would Bryan want to jump from there? At that point I realized where I was. I really looked at the dam for the first time and saw the huge sign embedded in the cement walls: "DANGER, DO NOT GO IN THE WATER, UNDERTOW." My dream had been a warning–a warning and a reminder to cover my son with prayer.

"Mother, I'm so sorry. It was an accident," Bryan began. "I just know I can get it if you'll let me dive in. My hands were wet when I cast and the rod slipped out of my hand, but I know I can get it. Just let me dive in," he pleaded. "I know it cost you a lot of money and I'm sure I can get it."

I dropped to my knees and began to cry as I held my son, for I knew in my heart that God had protected him.

"Don't you understand that nothing I own is worth your life, Bryan? Look at those signs, Son. They tell you it's dangerous. You don't know what's under that water, but the sign means what it says. I love you so much and I'm so thankful you didn't jump in. I could have lost you and I couldn't bear that. Please know that rod can be replaced, but you never can."

That was several years ago, and now here I was again, awakened from sleep and feeling compelled to pray for Bryan. Just as before, I didn't know why God was prompting me to pray now, but I remembered that previous time and the protection that had been put around my son at the dam. I knew the Spirit didn't awaken me without a reason, and I knew with certainty that this was serious.

I felt so humble that the Lord would surprise me with lights and heat, and yet I knew that this was a task to be approached with diligence. As before, my prayer was not lengthy or agonizing. I simply acknowledged that while I could not always watch over my son, I knew my Heavenly Father could, and it was into His hands that I placed Bryan that night.

The next day Bryan was leaving for another fishing trip, this time at a park near Troy, North Carolina, a town a few hours away. I glanced out the window as Bryan was packing the car, and once more the words "Danger, Danger, Danger" drummed into my spirit. Looking for danger of an immediate nature, I scanned the driveway and surrounding area for snakes. We lived in the woods and it was not unusual to see copperheads around there, so snakes were the first danger I could think of. But I saw none. Still the strong feeling of danger would not go away. So, again as I had the night before, I dropped to my knees and began to pray softly for protection around my son.

"Father, please. Whatever Satan means for bad, Your Word says You will turn it to good. You cannot have my son, Satan," I stated emphatically with a holy boldness given to me through Jesus Christ. "In the name of Jesus, I bind you from his life. Father, give him extra angels of protection," I added as I finished my short prayer.

Only two short hours later, the phone rang.

There was no mistaking who was calling. Somehow a State Highway Patrol officer's voice is unmistakable. Fear gripped me again, for I knew immediately he was calling about Bryan.

"Mrs. Forrester?" he inquired.

"There's no Mrs. Forrester here, but I have a son named Bryan Forrester," I answered, actually trying to stall hearing words I didn't want to hear.

"That's why I'm calling, Ma'am. This is Officer Smythe from Troy, North Carolina. Your son has been in an automobile accident and we need you here as soon as possible."

Now there was no escaping reality and the questions any mother would ask began to tumble out. "How bad is he? Can you tell?" My words were urgent and I fought back tears. I needed to hear anything and everything he had to say.

"We don't know for sure at this time, Ma'am. We're still cutting him out of the car, but it looks serious."

I hung up the phone, dashed out to the car, and headed for the hospital where the officer told me they would take Bryan. As I arrived there, a Life Flight helicopter was just taking off from the hospital's landing site. Fearing the worst, I rushed over to the people who were still on the ground as the copter rose higher in the air.

"Who's in there?" I screamed above the sound of the rotors. "My son's been in an accident. I need to know if he's in there."

One of the hospital staff members took me aside as the noise of the helicopter receded.

"There's a boy in there who was in an accident. I can't give you his name, but he was a passenger in the car. His nose was cut off and they're taking him to Duke."

"My son would have been the driver," I said. "Where is he?"

"He's probably in the emergency room, Ma'am. I really don't know. You will have to go in and ask."

I flew towards the entrance as quickly as my feet would carry me. I remember that people were coming and going and it felt so crowded in that doorway, but I

189

was determined. As I emerged into the hallway, I caught sight of Bryan in a room off to my right. Ignoring everything, I rushed to his side. His head was covered in blood and even his pillow was blood-soaked. His eyes were glassy and I knew he didn't see me.

"You can't be in here," one doctor said. "You're not sterile."

Hardly hearing and not caring what he said, I placed my hand on my son and pleaded the blood of Jesus over him and asked for his healing. I knew that God would hear my prayer.

"You are going to be all right, Bryan. Do you hear me? God woke me up last night and warned me. He knew that this accident would happen and you are in His hands, and you will be fine."

There were doctors and nurses and medical personnel all around us, but I was totally oblivious to anyone else who might be listening. I only wanted my son to hear that God was in charge. Now that I had done everything I could do for Bryan at this time, I allowed myself to be gently escorted out to the hallway. The man who had accompanied me out had a very kind and compassionate face and gentle voice as he spoke to me.

"I know it looks really bad in there. That's one of the reasons we don't usually allow family members to come in. But let me explain to you what has happened. Bryan's scalp has been lacerated from front to back, but he's going to be okay. Head wounds always bleed very profusely, and it always looks worse than it is. He may have a slight hairline fracture, but his skull is intact and his brain is uninjured except for a concussion. The neck brace is a precautionary measure. We have to be sure there is no injury to his spine that could paralyze him or worse. Because of the way he was pinned in the car, we needed to cut his pants leg off to be sure that his leg hadn't been broken. It hadn't. He has lacerations, abrasions and bruising, but no broken bones. He's going to be all right. Do you hear me? He's going to be okay."

"Yes," I said. "And thank you for everything you're doing for my son."

I had heard what the doctor had said; I knew for a fact that he was going to be all right. He lay in that trauma room protected under the blood of Jesus and I knew he was going to be all right.

"We don't have any facilities for you to stay overnight, but I can arrange for a lawn chair for you if you want to stay with him."

"Of course I want to stay," I answered. "Thank you so much."

As he left to go back in to attend further to Bryan, I slumped against the wall in the hallway.

"I overheard the doctor talking with you," said a nurse as she came up beside me. "You're that boy's mother, aren't you?" she stated more than asked, sounding as if she already knew that I was.

"Yes," I replied.

"I won't keep you long because I know this has been very hard on you, but you need to hear this. I've worked at this hospital for twelve years. In all that time I have *never* driven down the street I took to work this morning. In fact, I don't even remember how I got on that street this morning. All I know is that I was there at your son's accident. I was the first one on the scene. I could see your son pinned in the car. The driver's side window was broken out, so I leaned in to see if there was anything I could do. I reached in to check and he wasn't breathing. I crawled in through the window as far as I could and gave him mouth-to-mouth resuscitation and he began to breathe again. I will never be able to understand why I was there, but I felt compelled to tell you that I was."

"Thank you," I told her. "Thank you for being there for my son. But let me tell you something. I know how you got on that street. It was God's answer to my prayer. You see, the Lord woke me up at two-thirty this morning and told me my son was in danger. My obedience when he told me to pray allowed one of His angels to get you where you needed to be today. I hope you will always remember this day and how the Lord used you. May the Lord bless you for what you've done."

As I waited to be allowed back in with Bryan, I knew in my heart why she had been on that unfamiliar street that morning. She was part of God's answer to my prayer. She was part of His protection plan for Bryan.

I called Bryan's father, who lived only one hour away, but he would not come to comfort his son.

Bryan was in and out of consciousness throughout the night as I kept my lawn chair vigil at his bedside. The next morning, I was blessed to have Bryan awaken. Surprisingly, he woke up quite bright and alert.

"I'm hungry," he stated matter-of-factly, looking over at me as if nothing had happened.

"Son, do you realize the seriousness of what has happened to you?"

"Yes, Mother, I know, and because I do know, I have to share something with you. Are the clothes that they cut off me in the emergency room here?"

"Yes, Bryan. I believe they are under your bed in a bag."

"Would you get them out, please?"

"Sure," I said, quite puzzled by his request. "But why?"

"I had a dream three nights ago," he began. "And in this dream, I was in a room just like the one in this hospital. I saw doctors and nurses in my dream and I recognized those same faces yesterday in the emergency room here. I don't know their names, but I recognized their faces, Mother. In the dream, I knew I'd been in an accident, but it felt like my right leg had been cut off. I didn't know if it had been broken or if it was cut off, so I raised my right foot to look at it. I wanted to see if I could see my foot. When I did, I saw that my new shoe that you had bought me was cut from the big toe to the heel. You remember the canvas shoes you bought me? It was like a razor blade had just cut it all the way through. Now I really need to see that shoe."

I immediately searched through the bag holding his personal items and found the shoe. As I held it up, we could both see that it had been cut exactly as Bryan described seeing it in his dream.

"Son. You have dreams like I do. They are prophetic dreams and you have a prophetic gift. Do you understand this, Bryan? You have a calling on your life and God continues to save you from the brink of death. You've got to understand when He shows you something this clearly, Bryan, that He's calling you. We'll keep this shoe and I pray it will always be a constant reminder to you. Take a good look at this shoe. This is real, Bryan. God has set you aside for a specific purpose. His hand is on you, son. He's calling you and you need to answer Him."

With wonder in my heart at the mysterious ways in which God works and a thankfulness that defies description, I sat back in my chair and just looked at my child. *Yes, Bryan,* I thought. *God has a very special plan for you and I will continue to pray that He will soon make that plan crystal clear to you. Until then, I will rest in the knowledge that you are kept in the hollow of His hand.*

# Chapter
## 24

# "A Sign Of The Dove" Is Born

The day I met Joanna was a turning point in my life. I didn't realize it the day I met her in Sunday School and she shared her Bible with me, but I quickly found out what kind of impact one person can make on our lives when God is involved.

The day after our Bible-sharing, I decided that I would really like to have a Bible like the one Joanna had. I'd never seen one quite like it and I had found it very helpful during Sunday School. I had noticed there was a Christian bookstore called "Sign of the Fish" in the small shopping mall across from my apartment. I had intended to drop in and look around the store, but had never gotten around to it. Today, however, I had a specific reason to stop in. I was going to find a Bible like Joanna's. But I found out that it was not as easy a task as I'd envisioned.

There were all kinds of Bibles displayed on shelf after shelf, but I was determined to find that special one. Finally, I literally sat down on the floor so I could look thoroughly through the Bibles I had pulled down. The longer I searched, the more frustrated I became. It seemed harder and harder to remember just what that Bible had looked like. I brushed back a strand of hair from my face and lifted my eyes slightly from the pages of the Bible I was holding in my hands. That's when I saw them. Directly in front of me was a pair of feet. Since I was sitting right in the middle of the aisle, I realized that I must be blocking the way. I scrambled to my feet and started to apologize, stopping in mid-apology when I realized who the person was. It was Joanna, the lady who had shared her Bible with me just a little over twenty-four hours ago.

"It's you!" I said, totally astounded that she would just happen to be in the same store at the same time. "I'm so glad you came in here today. I've been searching and searching for a Bible."

"I can see that," she said, looking at the Bibles that surrounded me on the floor.

"Oh, but what I'm looking for is one like yours. Would you mind showing me that Bible you were using on Sunday?" Without hesitation, she reached out and plucked a Bible off a nearby shelf.

"It's this one," she said, handing me the Bible.

"This is just great! I really liked the way it read, and I couldn't find it. Then you came in. I can't believe I ran into you!"

A sweet smile crossed her face.

"Do you work here?" I said, realizing that she seemed even more at ease in the store than a casual customer might have been.

"Well, yes I do," she responded. But again, that smile said more.

"You own this store, don't you?" I asked, suddenly quite sure of what her answer would be.

"Yes, I do," she responded.

Over the next few months, I got to know her better and became fascinated with her knowledge of the books and the easy manner she had with the customers. What I saw was a business and a ministry combined, and I was hooked. I now knew that I wanted more than anything to own a Christian bookstore. That first meeting was almost thirty years ago. We've spent time apart, but we've remained friends ever since.

It was five years after I met Joanna that a deteriorating marriage sent me back to her. This time I wasn't looking for a Bible. I was looking for a job. Joanna knew I wanted my own store but she also knew that I wasn't ready. She gave me a management position and made me promise to work for her for at least one year. I agreed and I stuck to my agreement, but it proved to be a hard year in many ways.

I had so much to learn, especially about managing people. When a person has been abused, physically, emotionally or verbally, as I had been, the hurt caused by that abuse will come out in many ways. I compensated for the pain of my abuse by utilizing a harsh, demanding tone that I thought would not allow anyone to question my authority. I had accepted a strong controlling spirit that I hid behind the beautiful story-telling gifts my Heavenly Father had given me. People loved to listen to my stories, but I also learned to use this ability to manipulate others. Can you imagine what that behavior smells like to other people, whether they are Christian or not? Well, I think it would be like sprinkling sugar on skunk fumes.

Just think about it. Have you ever driven down the highway and driven past where a skunk was hit by a car and the odor envelopes your car? I guarantee that smell will have you opening the windows, running the air conditioner and doing anything else you can think of to get rid of it, but that stench can overpower just about anything. That's the way the spirit of rejection works. It seizes the opportunity to seep into the personality of an abused person. The irony is that the person who has been abused often becomes abusive in one way or another. It's a coping mechanism. It's logic gone wrong. The spirit of rejection can manifest itself in many ways, but its goal is always to continue to cause pain. Some people compensate for feelings of rejection with overeating and self-deprecating humor. Some become bitter and lash out at others. Some become controlling and manipulative, thinking that being in control is the same as being accepted.

However this spirit shows itself, it ultimately is like sprinkling sugar on skunk stench, because no matter how sweet the sugar is, it can never overcome the stink of a skunk. The smell of the skunk always prevails, especially if the spirit of rejection is operating through the area of your spiritual gifts. In my case, I am an accomplished storyteller, but my gift was not bearing fruit and a tree with no fruit is as a clanging cymbal. I think about the priests in the Bible whose robes had bells and pomegranates sewn onto the hem. When they walked in areas of the temple that only the priests could go, the people would know they were still alive by the sound of the bells. Between the bells hung the "fruit," which actually were large, multicolored balls called pomegranates, after a fruit of the region. If the pomegranates had not been placed between the bells, the result would have been a harsh, clanging sound, which would have been an offensive sound in the house of God, rather than the sweet clarity of the individual bells harmonizing with each other as the priest walked.

Spiritual gifts that are abused bear no fruit and are like bells without pomegranates. They fall on the ears of the people with a harsh clanging sound, and that is how I was coming across to people at that time. But God is so good. If you want to be healed, He will give it to you in increments when He knows you just can't take it all at once. I know, because that's the way He began to heal me.

Most of the employees in the store that I managed were young ladies who were still in high school, or in their first or second year of college. When I took over as manager, I was stepping into a store that was trying to recover from the embezzlement actions of the previous manager. It's always easier to see Satan's cunning methods when we look back on how he pulled someone else into sin. There is a strong element of control in a job where you must manage other people. Satan likes to convince you that it's just your job. You may never see it coming when he draws you over the line from competent managing into submission to a controlling spirit.

The sweet young people who were now under my management had been wrongly instructed by the previous manager. They had developed many bad habits and had been encouraged to participate in dishonest practices. For example, they had often clocked in for the manager in the morning, allowing the manager to show up four or five hours late. The manager would then arrange a reward for their assistance, which would often be unrecorded time off for that employee, thus compounding what had already been stolen from the store's owners.

So I saw my new job as two-fold. I needed to get the store back on track and I needed to make these employees understand that the training they'd received before was wrong. I wanted to save them, to redirect them to the things of God, and I did so by exposing error to them on a one-on-one basis. But unfortunately, I was still not fully healed. Remember? I had skunk stench mixed with my sugar. Sadly, I lost a few of these employees before I realized that my uncontrolled sharp tongue was getting in the way of their healing and of mine. Over the next year, God began to show me my error, as well as theirs. Thanks to His goodness and patience, by the time I left one year later, the sugar was growing and the smell of skunk was diminishing. Gifts without fruit...what a sad state. But what an awesome thing it is when you can see the first few little buds on your fruit tree.

Now that I had some experience in managing a Christian bookstore, I felt I was ready to pursue my dream of owning my own store. I found a building to rent, which had been split up by multiple office cubicles. My two sons came in to help and together we pulled down walls and scraped up tile off the floor. Everyone should try this at least once. It was invigorating, to say the least, but it is also a very humbling experience.

As we were winding up our reconstruction efforts, I was driving back to the store when I saw a sidewalk artist spray painting T-shirts. I quickly pulled over and stopped my car.

"Hi!" I said as I climbed out of the car. "I was just wondering if you could paint a dove and bring out its comforting qualities by soft colors and shadows."

"Yep, I sure can," he responded without hesitation.

"Well, let's see your work." I handed him some money and he began to create the dove I requested. It was perfect. The dove hovered in a cloudy mist and it was just what I needed to see.

"Can you spray paint a ceiling with billowing clouds?" I asked.

"Yes I can," he said.

"Then pack up your stuff," I told him. "You're hired."

I had another young artist already working on creating large renditions of the angels Michael and Gabriel. My intent was to suspend these flying angels in the corners of the store–Michael with his sword flying in the clouds over the books and Gabriel, blowing his horn, over the music section. Things were beginning to fall into place.

I also had a vision of a stained glass dove, flying through the clouds, which I would hang in the front window, but I didn't know anyone who could do it the way I saw it in my mind. I knew of one company, which I had used for a window in my home, but their work wasn't the type I needed. I was sure that the Lord would provide the answer when the time came, however. I had a gentleman by the name of Mark Capps working on the design of the dove and when it was ready, I would need a special stained glass artist. For the time being, I would wait and attend to other things.

I needed fixtures for my new store and I had no idea what that would cost, so I began to investigate by going to a warehouse that sold used store fixtures. At the time I visited, they only had one bookshelf that would be appropriate for my store, but it gave me an idea of how much each one would cost and how many books it would hold.

*Just how many four foot shelves would fit in my little store space?* I wondered. Math has never been my best subject so I had to find a way to calculate how many I would need and at the same time, see how to fit that number into my store. My two sons, Joseph and Bryan, and I decided to use large pieces of cardboard cut to the size of each book shelf. We laid them out on the floor in the empty store to get an idea of what it was going to look like. But then came the real problem. I didn't have enough money to get the number of shelves I would need, even at the one hundred dollars each the office warehouse was asking for used shelves. But I was going to need those fixtures, nonetheless.

I had gotten a small loan from the bank to buy books and so on, but thirty thousand dollars wasn't a great deal to start a new business with, and I would have to be very frugal. The day after my bank loan went through, I heard about an auction that was taking place. They would be selling all types of store fixtures. It was just thirty minutes away, so I headed for the auction site. I had never bid at an auction, but when I arrived I saw that there were many bookshelves just like I needed.

From my previous investigation, I knew that used shelves like these usually sold for between seventy-five and one hundred dollars, depending upon the condition. The auctioneer passed around a detail sheet with the fixtures enumerated on it. There were forty-five pieces in all, and I marked twenty with my pencil as those I would like to bid on. Soon it was time for the auction to start, and the first one was pulled out into the parking lot of the service station where the auction was being held. I took a deep breath, said a quick prayer, and bid five dollars. When my five dollar bid was acknowledged, it was as if an angel put all the other bidders to sleep, because not one person bid against me. Lot after lot was brought out and my bid of five dollars was the top bid for each of the twenty items I had marked on my sheet. As I checked off the last of the twenty items, more shelves were brought out for bid. Now, however, the crowd was awake again and the bids began climbing into the expected seventy-five to one hundred dollar range. I knew I had just been part of a miracle, and I thanked and praised God all the way home.

Now things really started moving. The next day I got a call from Mark, the artist who was drawing the design for the stained glass dove. The dove was ready, he said. I drove to his house, excited to see his drawing for the first time. He had drawn the perfect dove and I loved it except for one thing. He had made the feet of the dove to look like eagle's talons, ready to grab its prey.

"Mark," I said gently. "This is perfect except for one thing. In the Bible, we are told that the dove represents the Holy Spirit. He is our Comforter. He comes to teach us. You have this bird with the feet of an eagle like he's going to swoop down and get people."

"I thought that's what the Holy Spirit did," he responded.

"No. No. He's very peaceful, very comforting. So I must ask you to make his feet gentle as he comes down. It should be like the dove that hovered over Jesus' head when He was being baptized by John the Baptist."

"Oh! I can do that," he said. "Come back tomorrow. I'll have it fixed."

The next day, I drove to his house and it was absolutely perfect. I thanked Mark for his beautiful work and his willingness to make the change I'd requested, and headed home. I was just coming in the door when the phone rang. It was a friend of mine who was a doctor.

"Hi, Toni. This is Dr. Wilson. I'm calling you because there is a spiritual warfare conference being held in Durham and I know how interested you are in this subject. The conference speaker is Dr. Francis Frangipane who is an excellent warfare teacher, and I have an extra ticket. Would you like to go?"

"Oh, I would love it! Thank you so much."

"It's basically for counselors, doctors, and pastors, but I really think that it would do you some good."

"I really appreciate it. I'll come by your office and pick up the ticket."

The next morning I woke up, so excited about going to this conference that I had temporarily forgotten about the picture of the dove that I had left lying on the passenger side of my car. As I started to drive out of the driveway, I glanced at the picture. I often pray as I travel in my car, and seeing the dove lying there reminded me that this was a perfect time for prayer.

"Father. I'm just asking you today for a very special stained glass company to do this dove. The picture Mark has drawn is so perfect, and Father, the stained glass I had made before was not the same. It didn't have the right movement to the glass. This is such a special, special picture. Please send me the right stained glass company to do this picture. I thank You Father that You do answer my prayers and I praise You and I ask that You just open my ears and my spirit this morning to this teaching. I ask this in Jesus' name, Amen."

When I got to the conference, it was really exciting. I had read all of Dr. Frangipane's books and I was anxious to meet the author. Finally a gentleman came out on the stage, and I was sure he was about to introduce Dr. Frangipane.

"Will everyone that thought I was a woman, please raise your hand," he said.

What a way to begin a seminar! I have to admit I was one of the ones who had thought Francis Frangipane was a woman. I didn't know any men named Francis at that time, and I just assumed that the author was a woman. What I did see was that this man, Francis, was a very astute teacher.

After the morning session, Dr. Frangipane made an announcement that the hotel where we were meeting had closed the restaurant to other diners, and they were serving a buffet only for the people who were attending that day's conference. "I have a request," he continued. "Will you please not eat with the people you've been sitting with this morning, since you've had some opportunity to get to know them already. I would encourage you to walk up to a table of strangers, introduce yourself and make some new Christian friends."

I thought that was an excellent idea, so when I got my tray, I picked a large circular table for twelve. There were people already seated at the table, but I walked up to the one vacant chair and asked if anyone was sitting there.

"No. You're welcome to sit with us," one of them said. As I began to sit down, the lady seated directly across the table from me stood up and leaned forward, peering at my nametag.

"Toni. I recognize your name. You're the lady from Burlington that's trying to open a Christian book store...and doing so on a shoestring, I understand, or should I say, on a prayer. We've been praying for you in our prayer group."

"Really?"

"Yes," she continued. "And I'm the one who will do your stained glass dove."

"What?"

"Yes. My name is Regina and I do stained glass. We'll talk after the conference."

I was so totally surprised, I couldn't say anything else. I couldn't even eat. There was a lump in my throat. I realized that it had been only a few hours since I'd prayed for a stained glass artisan, and now here I was having lunch with the woman I knew in my spirit God had sent to perform just that task. I had never even seen her work, but I knew God had and I was assured that He had sent her to me. *Father*, I prayed silently. *You move so fast! Sometimes I'm almost afraid to pray, You move so fast. But I thank You and I know this is Your answer to my prayer. I can't wait to see her work!*

As soon as the meeting was over, Regina gave me her phone number and told me to give her a call. I handed her the picture of the dove that Mark had drawn so that she could study it. Soon thereafter, we met to go to a stained glass factory where, with Regina's guidance, I was able to personally select the pieces of glass that I wanted her to use. I chose an opalescent white for the wings so that when the sun came through it would show rainbows of color; then I selected a deep purple to represent royalty for the background color. I was sure it would be perfect, so I was more than a little surprised when Regina called me a few nights later. It was a phone call I'll never forget. Regina told me she had started on the dove, but as she began to lay out the purple glass I had picked out for the area surrounding the dove, she had to stop.

"I've been working on this dove and I know that it's anointed, but as I began to work with the purple background glass, I felt the Holy Spirit telling me 'whoose, whoose, whoose...Wind.' Then I realized what was wrong. Toni, this background glass you picked hasn't got any movement. Would you trust me to pick some other glass so that I can make ribbons of wind around the dove?"

"Absolutely," I responded, having learned long ago that listening to the Holy Spirit's prompting doesn't lead you in a wrong direction. "You have carte blanche. You do anything that you feel you need to do." Then I hung up, trusting the endeavor to Regina and the Holy Spirit.

Finally the day arrived when I saw the completed project for the first time. It was truly the most magnificent stained glass I have ever seen in my life. Regina had been right to listen. The whole piece had life and movement. I will always treasure the day Regina and her husband came in and hung it ever so carefully in my store's front window. It was awesome.

After the store opened, things moved quickly. I had been in the original location not much over a year when

I felt that it was definitely time to move. Let me explain. First, there had been a flood. Water had come from the building next door and flooded into my building. We mopped that up and were moving forward again when a tornado hit the end of the building and blew out the glass. After considering that I had already encountered a flood and a fury of wind, I felt it was time to move. The tornado had given me free publicity in the local newspaper, since I was the only store in the town that was hit, so I could easily announce my plans to move in the context of this storm. So on the heels of the flood and the tornado, I moved my store to a shopping center on the other end of town, and it was in this new location that the Lord taught me some very valuable lessons.

# Chapter
## 25

# The Hat Story

*I* always thought of my bookstore as a ministry as well as a business. For me, it was a place to reach out to people, to pray for them and to share with them spiritual truths I had learned. However, as I soon came to discover, it was also a place for me to be taught lessons by my Heavenly Father. One of the first lessons was given through my manager.

Deborah had stuck with me from the beginning. She had been with me through the flood and the tornado and the many ups and downs of starting a new business. Even though she had lost her husband and had gone through a long grieving period, she still stood by me and had been a wonderful employee and friend. Now she was the manager of my store at its new location. God had enabled me to prosper and the store was growing. I had added several part-time employees to the staff, which took some of the strain off Deborah and me.

One day shortly after the move to the new store, we were preparing a flyer that was going to be mailed out. It was time sensitive and had to go out that day. When I arrived at work that morning, Deborah was sitting at the desk. She was treasurer at the church we attended, and was writing checks to pay the church bills and using my stamps to stamp them. Now, in all fairness, before I continue I must tell you that Deborah is one of the most honest people I've ever encountered, so I knew she wasn't taking anything of mine by using the stamps. I also knew that she often came to work early to do the church bills at the desk. I had seen her do it many times before and I knew she was not working on my time since she had yet to clock in. But on this particular day, it irritated me that she was using my stamps. I had started watching how many stamps I was using at the store, and her using my stamps would throw off my count. Not only that, I'd have to go get some more and frankly, I just didn't have the time. Without so much as a hello, I confronted her.

"Deborah," I said sharply. "From now on, I would appreciate it if you would use the church's stamps for its bills, not mine. While I know you're not taking my stamps," I continued solicitously, "I would prefer it if you would just bring the church's stamps here and use them. When you use mine, it makes my store's usage count off."

"No problem," she responded politely. "I was going to pick up some stamps this afternoon when I got off work and replace them, but I'll be glad to use the church's stamps in the future. I'll just bring them in here and put them in the drawer."

"Thank you," I said flatly. Quite proud of the way I had handled the matter, I turned and walked out.

Later that afternoon, I had a large amount of flyers ready to go in the mail. They were not stamped because I had contacted a company that does mailings and they apply the postage for you. It's a bulk rate situation, and it's usually less expensive than buying the stamps at the post office. I had used this company before and had been very satisfied, so I had no doubt that this would go just as smoothly.

I had placed all the flyer sheets in a large cardboard box and dashed to the car so that I could get to the mailing company before they closed. As I drove, it began to rain. In fact, it began to rain very hard. With the rain pounding the roof of the car, I decided to pull right up to the door. I went around to the passenger side, got the box, covered it, and dashed inside. When I got to the counter, the gentleman there asked me how many pieces of mail I had. When I told him that I had 275 pieces of mail, he said it would be better for me to go to the Post Office because it was going to cost me more to use his service. He explained that I needed at least 300 pieces in order for it to be economical. Great! So, with the rain still pouring down, I trudged back out to the car, put the box in and got in myself.

Now, I'm on a short time limit because the Post Office closes at four o'clock, and it was ten minutes to four. I'm rushing and it's raining even harder. I'm about halfway to the Post Office when it happens. Without warning, the windshield wiper blade on the driver's side of the car flies off into a nearby yard. Straining to see through the downpour, I quickly pull over, park the car, and go into the soggy yard to pick up that pesky, but absolutely necessary, piece of rubber. I get back to my car and thread it back on to the windshield wiper frame.

Since I am out in this rain without a raincoat, I am now drenched. But I get in the car anyway and head for the Post Office. I pull the car to a halt in front of the Post Office just in time to see them put up the CLOSED sign. Now, that puts me in quite a fix. Here I am with all these dated materials that have to go in the mail before midnight and the Post Office is closed.

Beaten, I drive back to work. By the time I get there, the rain has stopped. *Of course*, I think. *Now that I couldn't care less if it's raining or not, it stops.* I pick up my box of flyers and carry them back in to the store. I'm not dry. I am not in a good mood and I look like a drowned rat. Deborah takes one look at me and says, "What in the world happened to you?"

"You're just not going to believe it," I tell her, shaking my head and talking as fast as I can out of sheer frustration. "You're just not going to believe it. First of all, the mailing place wouldn't take these flyers because there's only 275 pieces. Did you know we needed 300? No, of course not. Neither did I. Well, I didn't have 300, so I'm racing to the Post Office, but of course it's closed when I get there because the windshield wiper flew off the car and I had to retrieve it in the rain and that's how I got so wet, and...and..."

Deborah couldn't help smiling a bit and with a slight chuckle, she said, "No problem, Toni. It will be all right. On my lunch hour today, I went to the Post Office and picked up the church's stamps. Since I used yours this morning, I'll take the flyers home with me tonight and use the church's stamps on them. Then, I'll take them to the Post Office before midnight."

After all that, I started crying.

"Now what's wrong?" Deborah asked.

"Do you not see this? Do you not see this lesson that I'm standing here learning?"

"Actually, Toni, no. I don't. What is it?"

"Well I just got on to you this morning for using my stamps for the church's mail. Now you're going to use the church's stamps to save me. So what's wrong with this picture? I don't know what it is that makes me be this way. I am so sorry. Whatever this is that's on me, please pray that it will come off."

"Well, if you're really in a mood to listen, maybe Sonja and I could talk to you for a minute or so. There's something that we would really like to discuss."

"Okay," I said. "Let's talk. Since it's time to close the store, let's just talk."

I went back to my office and sat down. Deborah and Sonja soon joined me. "Okay, you two. What is it?"

"You know that we love you like a sister."

"Yes, it's evident that you love me."

"But sometimes, Toni, you just say things and they hurt us so badly. It's not that you're not right. It's more the way you say it."

"Well, explain it to me. Tell it to me like I say it. Say it to me."

"I can't," said Sonja.

"I can't either," Deborah agreed.

"Well, uh, how am I going to know what it is that I do if you don't tell me? How can I fix it if I don't know what it is?" After some thought, I spoke again. "I'll tell you what. I know that what you're saying is the truth because I see your sincerity. Apparently, I have hurt you both. Let me go home tonight and pray about it. If this is a character flaw or something in my personality that's causing pain to those I care about, I want to get it out and I want the Lord to heal me. So, just give me an evening. I've heard what you said. I've been hurting your feelings and it's something about the tone in my voice. Just let me go home and pray. Tomorrow morning, the Lord will give me a solution."

The next morning, with the Lord's solution in my hands, I went in to work. I took both Sonja and Deborah back in my office and said, "This is the plan." I had a hammer and a ten-penny nail in one hand and a hat that said JESUS IS LORD in the other. Now this was one ugly, camouflage-material baseball hat, but it made quite a statement. "I'm going to nail this nail behind the checkout up front," I said. "On this nail, I'm going to hang this hat. Now I don't want anybody to be embarrassed, but I do want to know when I've hurt you. So this is what we'll do. When we're work-

213

ing around here and I say something to you that's not Christ-like or that hurts your feelings in any way, all you have to do is go put the hat on. That will be the signal. When I see either of you wearing that hat, I'll know.

"I can take a look right then at what I've said or what I've done, and you won't have to say a word. You see, I think one of the things that's a problem is that when I do hurt your feelings and you try to tell me, I think you're arguing with me. So then I argue right back and my need to be heard gets stronger and stronger. I get lost in the argument and I don't see your problem. With the hat, nobody will have to say anything. Just seeing you wearing the hat should hit my spirit. So let's give it a try, okay?"

After the hat went up, I was on guard and put forth a special effort to be nice, so it took a while before the hat became necessary. It had been perhaps a week before one of them put the hat on, and then I can hardly tell you what it felt like. It hit my spirit dead center and all I could do was cry. I knew in my heart I was not intentionally hurting them, but my words and actions spun back at me in instant replay and I knew without a doubt that I had.

Whenever I think about that day, I think about how David must have felt when the prophet told him he was the one who stole the sheep that he used for his banquet. My sin and David's sin might not have been the same, but, I think the words of the prophet must have hit his spirit the same way that the Lord hit me when I saw that JESUS IS LORD hat. That day I became very aware of the tone of voice that I use to speak to people. It's taken a long time, but I think I'm on the other end of the spectrum now. I'm not saying that I don't ever speak sharply or in a hurtful manner. I think we all do at times. But now I try to stay very aware of the tone in my voice. I thank the Lord that He works on me in increments like He does. For me, one lesson at a time is just fine.

# Chapter
## 26

# Anointed With Oil

oes prayer make a difference? I believe it can and it does. I have seen the difference it can make many times in my life. It can even mean the difference between life and death. Let me give you an example.

It was a relatively ordinary day. I was out running errands for my store and was rushing, as usual. I had called in a tossed salad order in hopes of picking it up on my way back to my store, "A Sign of the Dove." As I pulled into the left turn lane, I was prompted to glance down at my gas gauge. It showed my fuel was nearing that dreaded "E" for Empty. I was actually more concerned about getting my lunch than I was about the status of the fuel in my car, but I couldn't afford to run out of gas either. There was a gas station close by, so I decided I'd better stop for the gas first. Besides, my salad wasn't going to spoil if I stopped now. Signaling for another lane change, I headed for the Amoco station about a mile ahead. I pulled in at the first pump, stepped out of my car, and began filling up.

It was a beautiful day and I stood there taking in the scenery while the gas gurgled into my tank. The Amoco was located on Huffman Mill Road, a four-lane highway with a cement median. Directly across from the gas station, I could see a side street that joined with Huffman

Mill Road. I noticed that a small car with two young boys inside had just pulled up to the stop sign. As they stopped, a loud roaring sound startled me. I turned my head to see what was making the noise and saw a large white truck approaching the intersection at a high rate of speed. The boys had already begun to pull out of the side road. There was a slight incline in the highway and I could tell that the boys could not see the approaching danger.

I felt as if I was watching everything happen in slow motion. As the truck crested the little hill, the boys were already pulling out into the first lane of Huffman Mill Road. Had the truck been going the posted speed limit, they would have been well into the second lane before the truck reached the intersection and he would have missed hitting them. But he was speeding and when he finally did hit his brakes, he hit them so hard that his truck tipped up onto the right two tires. The truck driver jerked the steering wheel to the left to compensate, which pulled the truck into the second lane where the boys now were. That truck hit that little car broadside and knocked the car across the cement median, across another two lanes of traffic, and into the parking lot of the Amoco station.

I sprinted to the car where I found both boys obviously badly injured. I quickly opened my anointing oil, which I carry on my key chain.

"Someone call an ambulance!" I screamed, as I began to anoint the passenger and pray. He had hit the windshield and was semi-conscious with what looked like foam in his mouth. Then I went to the driver, anointed him as well, and got on my knees. I asked God to send angels to hold that boy's insides in place as I felt he had internal injuries from the blow to his side. I prayed God would take what Satan meant for bad and turn it to good. I prayed that He would touch the families of these boys and make this accident a turning point for them to come to Him.

When I stood up and opened my eyes, there were about twenty-five people there. Since they had not made a sound while I was praying, I was shocked to see them. As soon as I stood up however, they rushed the car.

Using my loudest, most authoritative tone, I yelled, "Don't touch them. Do not take them out of the car. Wait for the ambulance!"

One quite large gentleman went to the passenger side and started to open the door. "I said, don't touch them," I reminded him sternly. He backed away as the ambulance turned in the drive.

Since I had witnessed the accident, I gave my name to the police officer who came to assess the accident. I don't know what he wrote, but I know that I was never called to answer any more questions.

Later that day, I could not get the accident out of my mind. I called the hospital emergency room and said I had witnessed a bad accident. I asked if someone could tell me about the condition of the two boys who had been involved. The lady politely told me that she was not allowed to give that information over the phone but that she could tell me one of the boys had been rushed to Duke Hospital. I knew immediately which boy it was. I knew it was the driver.

The next day was Sunday, and during Sunday School I asked the Pastor, who was also our class's teacher, if we could all pray for the two boys who had been hurt in the accident I witnessed. Again, prayers were lifted up for these two young men.

At our church, we had a praise time before the pastor was to preach. As the pastor approached the pulpit, he said, "I am going to do something a little different today. It seems one of our members witnessed an accident yesterday, and she asked for prayer for these two boys that she does not know. There is something else that she did not know and I'm about to tell her. The best friend of the father of the boy that was taken to Duke was in our Sunday School class this morning. I have just come from a meeting with him in my office. So now, Toni, you will hear the rest of the story.

"The entire family was called in and was told that Jason was being rushed to Duke and that he was not expected to live. His spleen had exploded on impact and they did not know how much internal bleeding had occurred. But they did know that he was not stable at the time the family was notified. As the family gathered in the waiting room at Duke Hospital in Durham, North Carolina, they truly feared for Jason's life. Finally, Jason's doctor came out to speak with them. He told them that he really couldn't explain it, but it was like something was holding back the internal bleeding. He said that Jason had lost his spleen but that he seemed to be recovering by the minute. Someone who was there with the family said, 'That is what the lady said! The lady that was on her knees praying. She asked for angels to hold his insides.'"

When the pastor finished reporting "the rest of the story," there was no doubt in that congregation that morning that prayer makes a difference. I not only found out who the boy was that I had prayed for, but Jason's mother had found me. She and other family members came to my store periodically to report on his condition and we were all blessed. Do you remember what else I prayed for Jason? I had prayed that God would take what Satan meant for bad and turn it to good, that He would touch the family and make the accident a turning point for them. God heard *ALL* my prayer, because one of the reports I got on Jason's progress included the fact that the entire family had given their lives to the Lord and were in church every Sunday.

I have prayed over a lot of highway tragedies in my life. This was the first one that the Lord let me know how my prayers made a difference. You may not know the person's name and you may never know the outcome, but I believe prayer opens up a highway straight to Heaven that God in His love can answer. I believe a lack of forgiveness hinders prayers, so pray with a clean heart. Otherwise, why would the Scriptures warn us, as they do in Matthew 5:23 and 24, "Therefore if thou bring thy gift to the altar, and there rememberest that thy brother hath ought against thee; Leave there thy gift before the altar, and go thy way; first be reconciled to thy brother, and then come and offer thy gift." (Matthew 5:23,24 KJV) I believe this is an example to show us how important it is to stay repentant and forgiving because you never know when you might need a prayer answered during your day.

# Chapter
## 27

# *The Gay Bar*

When the Lord begins to clean you up and you know that you are yielding to Him, and you know that there's some progress, it frees you up to start praying to go deeper. So it was with me. It was during the summer of 1996 that I started praying to the Lord to show me His Glory.

"You know, Father," I prayed. "You showed Yourself to Moses and I know that Your Glory followed the tabernacle. And Father, that interests me. You know that I'm scientifically inclined. I've always loved science. I need to feel and touch and know what makes something work. I know there's more to Your Glory than what I can understand, so I'm asking You to teach me what Your Glory does, what it means and how I can receive it."

A series of events began to happen after I prayed this prayer that would lead to an answer, but just as in the other times the Lord has moved for me, I didn't realize I was in the lesson until the end. He has a process with me, which I suspect he uses with many other people, as well. He takes me through an experience and then backs me up so I can see what makes it tick. At this time in my life, the Lord had been waking me up often very early in the morning. This particular time, He woke me up at three o'clock in the morning. Those of you who sleep during this time of the night may not know this, but

221

there's often very good preaching scheduled late at night. In fact, there's a wonderful praise program on TV, so I picked up the TV remote and started searching, searching, searching.

"What do You want me to see? What do You want me to see?" I asked as each channel flew by. I knew from past experience that I would know it when I saw it, and I fully expected it to be some priceless gem of spiritual teaching. Suddenly, I stopped changing channels and stood riveted in place. This was not a Christian channel as I had expected. It was a newscast!

The first thing that caught my eye was the yellow crime tape that goes up so quickly around a crime scene, such as a murder. Then I heard the words: '...Bombing of gay bar–Atlanta.' I caught just that much of it and my eyes were now glued to the TV. Suddenly, I saw Joseph. My son was at the scene and was talking with a reporter who was interviewing him. It seems that they suspected that the bombing may have been carried out by the same person who bombed the Olympics and an abortion clinic.

Now someone has bombed the bar where Joseph's friend Bobby was manager. Joe had gone over that evening to help out his friend because he was short-handed. Now, I'm watching my son being interviewed. Thankfully, I can see that there are no wounds and that he does not appear to be hurt. I watched that newscast over and over and over again until about five in the morning, at which time I finally went back to bed. At six o'clock, the phone rang.

"Hi, Mom. It's me." I was so glad to hear Joseph's voice. "I'm just calling you because I didn't want you to get up and hear the news."

"Stop right there, Joseph. I've been watching you since three o'clock this morning, son."

"Of course. I should have known. God woke you up, didn't He, Mother? I was scared that if you got up and just heard the news without knowing I was okay, you'd have a heart attack."

"I probably would have, son. I probably would have. But God prepared me. I want you to know that I'm coming to Atlanta. Just as soon as that mess is cleaned up, I'm coming there because I want to see where you work. You know that I love you and these things are scary, so just prepare for a visit."

"That'll be fine, Mom. I would love to have you come."

I don't know how much time passed before I planned my trip, but when I got to Atlanta, it was late in the afternoon and I drove straight to the bar. When I arrived, Joseph came and greeted me. Then he took me around and introduced me to everyone in the room. They have a stage where they put on a floorshow. Backstage is a dressing room where the performers prepare for the show. I knew that they would be presenting a show where the men were dressed in drag, but some of Joe's friends came and got me and asked me if I would like to see what backstage was like.

I went back with them and discovered that it was not what one might expect. There was no nudity or anything of that nature. They were just putting on makeup, getting costumes ready and such. It was really quite interesting. They were very talented as makeup artists and while I was backstage, I just watched and listened to the things that they were saying and the way that they were talking. It was no different than watching any other actors prepare for a show. They were very kind to me and respectful. They asked if I would like a touchup with my make-up and I said yes.

When I went back out front, Joseph said, "You look much better, Mom. You look refreshed. You appeared very tired from your trip before."

Then Joseph escorted me to my front row table near the stage, and I began watching the acts performing that night. Joe would come to my table off and on because I was sitting alone and he wanted to make me feel more comfortable. But then a strange thing started happening.

Young men began to come up to my table. With tears rolling down their faces, they thanked me. They thanked me for loving my son enough to come into a gay bar. They told me they knew that I did not approve of the gay lifestyle, but that they could also see that I loved my son. Some told me they were dying of AIDS and only had a few months to live. Some said that their parents had banished them years ago, and that they would probably die alone. I don't have the words to tell you how this struck my heart. I know that the Lord does not want us to judge and that was what they reaffirmed when they said, "We don't feel judgment from you."

"It's not my place to judge you," I told them. "You have made your choices and you are living with the consequences of those choices. But know this, God and His forgiveness are available to you. Remember the story of the repentant thief on the cross beside Jesus the day Jesus died. In the last moments of that thief's life, he asked forgiveness and it was given to him. At any time in your life, you can have total forgiveness. Don't ever forget that."

"Well, we just want to thank you for the love that we see in you. You are the example we would like to remember of a true Christian; one that doesn't judge."

# Chapter
# 28

# Lady With A Gun/Glory

It wasn't long after I came home from Atlanta, that my lesson continued. I was in my store one morning when a lady came in the door. I walked to the front of the store to greet her and I could see that she had been crying, as her eyes were very puffy and red. I never push a customer to talk when I see that they are emotionally upset. I just try to keep my conversation light and see where God will lead.

"I don't believe I've ever seen you in here before."

"Oh, I've never been in here," she said. "As a matter of fact, I didn't even know this store was here. I was riding down Church Street and just felt compelled to come in here."

"Well, let me take you on an adventure," I offered. "I read five books at a time. Come with me. Let me show you some good books."

I turned my back to her and began to walk away, leading her further into my store. As I turned, I began to pray under my breath.

"Father, You know why she's hurt and You know what's hurt her. Please lead me to the right book to put in her hands."

The woman seemed rather anxious and I was fearful I didn't have much time, so I bent down, picked up a book and put it in her hands.

"Give me just a second. Let me walk around the corner here and look at another shelf," I told her.

"No. I'll take this one," she said and she placed the book on the checkout counter.

I went behind the cash register and checked her out. As she left, I asked her to please come back and let me know what she thought of the book.

It was about two in the afternoon when she walked back through the door.

"Do you remember me from this morning?" she asked. Her eyes were even more swollen now.

"Yes, I certainly do."

"Well, I've just come in here to tell you that the book you laid in my hands has changed my life, and I know now that Jesus loves me. What you didn't know was that on the front seat of my car there was a 45-caliber pistol, loaded. I was driving to the river. I was going to just sit on the bank and blow my brains out."

Although quite stunned by her words, I managed to respond, "Well, I'm so thankful that you came in here and I'm so thankful that it was the right book for you. Please come back. I would love to show you some more things. You are very right, you know. It was *not* a coincidence that you came in here. God really does love you and you must have a purpose, because He saved your life today. There is something He has for you to do, so please come back and see me. We can talk anytime."

I hugged her and sent up a silent prayer of thanksgiving to a God who knew just what she needed and who had allowed me to be a part of His plan for her. I saw her many times after that and I was able to watch as God continued to work in her life. To this day, I cannot tell you the title of that book. I don't even know what the cover looks like. So many people have asked me what book I gave that lady. I have to answer I don't know. God just put it in my hands to give her.

It had been only a few hours since the lady left that day when I got a phone call from Joseph.

"I'm coming in tonight, Mom. Will you do shrimp and lobster like you always do?"

"Sure, I will. What's the occasion?"

"I just need to escape, Mom. I'm just coming because I want to see you. I'm on the road now."

"I'll have supper ready when you get here. I'm so glad you're coming to visit."

What a delightful surprise! I told my employees that I was going to leave early because Joe was coming in unexpectedly, and I had to get to the grocery store. I went to Winn Dixie because they will steam the shrimp for me. I've found that I tend to overcook them and they wind up resembling leather, so I let the professionals do it. I ran in the store quickly, got the shrimp and lobster, went home and prepared the dinner.

Joseph was only there for one night, but we had a wonderful evening. I had to be at work early the next morning and Joe wanted to sleep late, but he said he would be by the store to see me before he left.

It must have been around ten in the morning when the same gentleman who waited on me at the meat counter in Winn Dixie the night before walked through my front door.

"I can't believe it," I said, delighted that he had stopped by. "I've been trying to get you in my store for a year. What was it? Did I buy enough pounds of shrimp, or what was it?"

"No. You're a good customer, that's for sure, but that's not why I'm here. Actually, I'm on my way to work and I really don't have time to shop with you today, but I can tell this is a wonderful store. I will be back, I promise. There is something I have to tell you, though. I'm just not sure that you will believe it."

"Oh, I'll believe you. Go ahead. Tell me. What is it?"

"You know when you came in the store last night?"

"Yeah."

"Do you remember that little white guy that was standing beside me at the meat counter?"

"Yeah, I remember him."

"Well, in case you don't believe me, I want you to know he's working today. You can come in the store and ask him because he saw the same thing I did."

"Saw what?"

"Well, when you rounded the corner, pushing your grocery cart back toward the meat department, I punched him and said, 'Look! Do you see what I see?' You glowed like a glow worm glows at night."

"Really?"

"I'm telling you that's the truth. And I told him that's not the first time you'd come in there glowing like that."

"Why didn't you pull me over to the mirror in the meat department and let me see?" I asked him excitedly. Then I thought about it a moment. "I'm sorry," I continued. "I didn't mean that. I wasn't meant to see. You were meant to come in here and tell me. Please excuse me. I didn't mean any disrespect. I appreciate so much your being obedient to the Lord and coming and telling me this. You see, He's been teaching me something recently. Now I believe I'm going to find out what it is, and I'm going to find out what it means. I often tell my friends that God takes me through a teaching, and then He backs me up to show me what it means. I just want to thank you. I really can't thank you enough for coming in here."

That night, the Lord woke me up again...at least I think He woke me up, because I don't know for sure if I was awake or asleep. I sat up in the bed and at the end of my bed there was a scene that was certainly not the opposite wall in my bedroom. It was like having a huge TV screen and watching a movie. The movie was "Independence Day©." There is a scene where they show an alien ship that had crashed years ago. The Army had put it into a hidden underground hangar and had repaired it. Now our planet was under attack by more aliens and we were looking for a solution. They believed that if they could get this alien ship to fly, they could fly it inside the aliens' mothership and blow it up. Without guidance from this orbiting command post, the aliens would be defeated. There was, however, a problem.

As the scene unfolds, two men are discussing the problem and one of them tells one of the soldiers, "Take your pistol. See that Coke® can? Fire your pistol at that Coke® can."

The soldier argues and says, "Sir, we're in a hangar. I can't fire my pistol in here."

"Just do what I said and fire at that Coke® can." As soon as he does, *WHOOM!* This blue shield comes up around that space ship. It was then that I heard the voice of the Lord say to me, "That is like My Glory."

"I see!" I said. "It's like a shield of protection...impenetrable."

"Right!"

Then the scene continued. One of the guys has a laptop computer and the other guy is asking, "Now how are we going to get into the ship?"

"Just wait a minute," says the guy with the laptop. "I'm going to put a virus into this computer, and then we'll download it into the ship's computer and it will break the shield. Watch."

He again instructed the soldier to fire at the Coke® can and this time, there was no shield protecting it. The shot ricocheted off the can and the can itself went flying. Now they could get into the ship and use it.

Just then the Lord spoke and said, "That's what happened in the Garden of Eden when the sin virus came in to Adam and Eve. It broke the shield."

"No wonder they hadn't needed clothes to protect them. They were clothed in Glory. That was their shield. I really understand it now. Now I know what the Glory is for. It's a protection to walk in!" Giving this idea further thought, I then asked, "But Lord, how do I get there?"

And He said, "You already did.

"*First:* Judge no man. When you went in the gay bar, you did not judge.

"*Second:* Listen to My voice. Be obedient. When you reached down and got that book, you were obedient.

"*Third:* Stay repentant."

Every day we should ask the Lord to forgive us. Every day, we should stay repentant. Every minute we think about it and every time sin is brought to our minds, we should ask right then for forgiveness. This was a great lesson for me. I hope it will be a great lesson for you, too.

# Chapter
# 29

# *Answered Prayer*

$\mathcal{I}$t was February and cold, almost time for Valentine's Day, when I got the call from my brother.

"Sis, they've just taken Dad to Memphis by ambulance. He's had a heart attack. It's bad. Can you get home?"

"I'm on my way right now."

My Dad's health had not been good for some time. Still, this heart attack was unexpected. I threw a few things in a suitcase, called my son Bryan, and asked him if he would go with me. Bryan was working in the mountains of North Carolina, and I had to drive through that area in order to go home. Arrangements were made to have one of his co-workers take care of Bryan's truck and I would pick him up in Asheville.

By the time I reached Asheville, it was quite late. The weather was horrendous and there were tornado warnings out all over, so we decided to check into a motel. My prayer in my room that night was simple.

"Lord, please let me get there in time. Let me get to the hospital for my Dad."

The next morning Bryan and I were up bright and early. The weather was still not very good, but having

Bryan in the car made me feel better. I was also very glad to be alone with him so we could talk. Bryan is a very quiet young man and he doesn't talk very much, but we chatted off and on during the trip and I found that comforting.

The entire trip, I had been concerned that I would not get to Memphis in time, but surprisingly we pulled into the Methodist Hospital parking lot at exactly the same time as the Blytheville ambulance bearing my father arrived. There was no way that an ambulance leaving Blytheville, which was only one hour away from Memphis, would be arriving now, twenty-four hours later. What could possibly have happened? I was sure my brother had told me that the ambulance had already left when he called me yesterday. *I'll figure out why later,* I thought. *Right now, I want to see my Dad.*

They had just pulled his stretcher out of the ambulance when I reached him.

"How's my Valentine?" I asked my father, still amazed that I had arrived at the same time he had. They took Daddy into a room and the entire family was there, with Daddy's wife Irene, her son and his wife, my brother and his wife, and Bryan and me.

My brother then explained that the ambulance had not left Blytheville yesterday because there were no rooms in the Memphis hospital. Daddy had spent the night in Blytheville. The ambulance had left today instead, which explained why we arrived at exactly the same time.

I had brought my Dad a big monkey with a great big red heart that I had gotten for him for Valentine's Day. Now I was bringing it to him at the hospital instead. It was a funny stuffed animal that talked and sang. The nurses got him and showed him to everybody, so he ended up cheering up a lot more people than just my Dad. But the very best gift was the one the Lord had arranged for me. It was the answer to my prayer. I was not only able to get to the hospital; the Lord arranged it so I was able to be there the minute my dad arrived.

The doctor came in and told us that Daddy would need to have open-heart surgery. They would be transporting Daddy to Baptist Hospital the next morning for the surgery. He told us all not to come back to Methodist Hospital the next morning because Dad would already be at Baptist. There was a family area there where we could wait for results from the operation. We all stayed that day and visited for as long as we could. Then we left to eat dinner. We all checked into a motel a short distance from the hospital and went to bed early, knowing that we were supposed to be at Baptist around eight in the morning. Surprisingly, I was able to sleep.

At three o'clock in the morning, I woke up. I felt prompted to go back to Methodist Hospital right then. Bryan was in the other bed next to me, so I got up very quietly and tiptoed in the bathroom to refresh myself and dress. I didn't want to wake him up, and I knew he could ride to the hospital later with my brother, who also had a room in the same motel. However, Bryan did wake up, which really surprised me, as he is usually a very deep sleeper.

"What are you doing?" he asked, noticing that I was up and dressed.

"I'm going to the hospital," I replied.

"Mother, did you hear what the doctor said when we were in Granddaddy's room last night? He said not to come back there–to go to Baptist."

"I know what he said, son. But I think my Daddy may be afraid and I'm going to go sit with him."

At that, Bryan slung the covers off the bed and stomped around on the floor looking for his jeans.

233

"What are you doing?"

"I'm getting dressed."

"Son. You don't have to go with me. I'm going by myself."

"Oh, no," he replied. "You'll get lost. It's dark. I can just see you getting lost, and then you'll be mad at me because you're not there when he's being operated on."

"Bryan. I covered five states in my job, son. I drove all up and down the East Coast. If I could find those businesses, I think I can get to that hospital."

"No, you can't," he insisted. "I know you can't. I'm going with you."

"Well, that's great, but please don't go with that attitude. If you want to go with me, fine. But I want Daddy to see a good attitude."

He finished dressing and we drove to the hospital. When we got there, Daddy's face lit up like a light bulb.

"What are you doing here?" he asked.

"Oh, we just came to sit with you, Daddy, until the ambulance comes to get you."

"Well, that's great," he said.

About that time, a little nurse came in the room to give Daddy one of those "la-la" shots. After she gave him the shot, she said, "Mr. Lewis. Now I'm going to be your girlfriend today, and I'm going to ride with you in the ambulance over to Baptist, and I will be riding back with you over here."

I saw Daddy's eyes get as big as saucers and he looked at her and he said, "You're going to move me after the operation? Please don't do that. Can't I stay at Baptist? I don't want to be moved."

"Oh, Mr. Lewis. It will be all right, I assure you. There are no rooms at Baptist. You'll see when you get over there. There are people on gurneys lining the hallways. They are packed over there. There is no way that you or anyone else is going to get a room in that hospital."

Once again Daddy pleaded, "Please. Please, can't they make some special allowance?"

"Sir. It really will be okay."

I saw Daddy's fear and I couldn't stand it. I looked at the nurse and said, "Ma'am, I know you know your job and I do not doubt for one minute that that hospital is loaded and overcrowded. But I want you to know that I am going to go to an authority higher than the hospital and this day, you will see a miracle. My father *will* have a room in Baptist Hospital." Turning to my father, I continued. "Now Daddy, look at me. Do you hear what I'm saying? You *will* have a room in that hospital. You will *not* be brought back over here. Daddy, believe with me. Believe with me."

"Oh, I've seen you do this before, girl," he said, looking visibly relieved "I believe you. Okay. I do believe you."

The nurse just shook her head and left the room. By now, the shot was beginning to take effect. Daddy is like Bryan. Neither one of them is a real talker, but that shot loosened him up. He began to tell stories. He told stories about the war. Then he told Bryan a story that he had never heard. He told my son how he had adopted me and what kind of early life I'd had. Tears rolled down Bryan's face as Daddy was telling him this. Then the most awesome thing happened...I watched my father bless my son.

It's very important for a male child to be blessed. The Bible has many stories of blessings. For example, there is the story of where Jacob stole the blessing from his brother, where Jacob blessed his two grandchildren, and now, this day, I was privileged to watch as my father blessed his grandson. He told him what a fine young man he had become. He told him how proud he was of him. He told him what a good son he was to take care of his mother.

I watched Bryan's face. This was something he had never heard from his own father. Most of Bryan's life he had been given only very negative things, mostly by his father's wives. One thing he had never received before was a blessing. Now I knew why I had been awakened at three in the morning to come and see my Dad. Now I understood why Bryan woke up, and why it was so important that he came with me. I saw that everything was unfolding exactly as God had intended.

Soon after Dad drifted off to sleep, they came to take him to the ambulance. Bryan and I got in my car and drove to Baptist. When we got there, we found the family waiting area. It was a huge room with space for many family members. Some people wait for long periods of time as their loved ones struggle between life and death. Quite a few people had even brought air mattresses so they could sleep on the floor. Each patient was represented by two or more family members that day. There were eight telephones on the wall, and when a patient came out of the operating room, the hospital staff would page the family's name. Then all the family had to do was pick up one of the phones and they would be updated on that patient's status.

When I walked in the room, my dad's wife, Irene was there with one of her sons, my brother and his wife. I walked up to my brother and I slid my hand in his hand.

"Where have you been?" he asked obviously surprised that I had not arrived sooner.

"I went to Methodist," I answered him.

"What did you do that for?"

"Because I wanted to. I was awakened in the middle of the night and I felt like Daddy might like some company, so I went to Methodist to be with him. I think he enjoyed it." Pausing, I looked at my brother, then continued. "I need you to do something with me, Harold. I need you to go someplace with me."

"Sister. Do you see this room? Do you see those eight phones over there on the wall? I'm not going anywhere. This is the important place to be. This is where they call you if anything goes wrong, or when they come out of their operating room–whatever. Those phones ring and they page you."

"Harold, Jr. This is *not* the most important place to be. I'm ten years older than you and if you don't go with me, let me tell you what I'm going to do. I'm going to fall down on this floor. I'm going to roll around like I'm having a seizure. I'll foam at the mouth if I have to. But know this, when I do, everybody in this room is going to look at you. So I'm telling you, you will either go with me or I'm going to do that. Do you want to be embarrassed?"

He studied me carefully, "You *would* do that, wouldn't you?" he said finally.

"I would," I stated firmly. "And I would do it because this is important."

"Okay. Let's go. Where are we going?"

"Just come with me. It's a very short distance."

We walked down the hall to the chapel. It was really a beautiful room. It had a huge stained glass window and a kneeling bench, and it gave me a feeling of peace just to enter it. No one else was there when Harold, Jr.

and I arrived so we walked up to the bench and knelt down.

"Now listen very carefully to me," I said. "All I want you to do is agree with me. We are Daddy's two children. It says in the Bible 'That if two of you shall agree on earth as touching any thing that they shall ask, it shall be done for them of my Father which is in heaven.' (Matthew 18:19 – KJV) And I know it's within His will for our father to be protected and for this operation to be successful. So if you will just say, 'I agree,' that's all you have to say. Okay? Okay.

"Father, I just come to you right now and I just ask you to intervene in this operation. Father, I'm asking for angels to be in the operating room to guide the doctor's hands."

"I agree," my brother said.

"And Father, I'm going to ask one more thing, please. When he comes out of the operating room, Father, I would ask that You provide a room for him here at Baptist."

"Sister," my brother interrupted. "Have you not seen the people on the stretchers in the hall? There are no available rooms in this hospital. They told us that before we ever got here. He's not going to get a room."

"Now look at you, Harold, Jr.! All I asked you to do was agree with me. Now I'm going to have to start all over again. Do you understand? All I want you to say is 'I agree.' So don't talk like that. Daddy *will* have a room here. Now I'm going to start all over and you're going to agree with me in prayer. Okay? Okay."

"Father, please excuse my brother's lack of faith. Today show him a miracle. Father, I'm asking one more time. Please, when Daddy comes out of the operating room, will You give him a room here at Baptist?"

"I agree," said my brother.

"Thank you. And thank You, Father, that You go before us before we even ask, and we thank You that this has already been prepared. Father, I honor You and I adore You. You are a mighty God. In Jesus' name I pray, Amen."

Then we left the chapel and walked back to the family room to join the other family members. It was another two hours of waiting before they finally announced 'Lewis Family' and gave the number of the telephone. Of course, Harold, Jr. beat me to the phone. After all, he's younger. But I was right beside him and had my head poked right up under his arm as he picked up the phone, and I listened carefully as he spoke to the doctor.

"It was a successful operation?" he said. "Doctor, we just thank you so much. He's breathing better than he was when he went in? That is terrific! Excuse me? He's in Room 345? O...kay. And we can go to his room now? Wonderful! Yes, sir. Thank you so much."

As my brother hung up the phone, he looked at me and said "Sister, I never doubted it for a minute."

"Good, Harold, Jr. I told you the Lord would show you a miracle today, and He has."

# Chapter
## 30

# *The Embezzler*

*J*ust about everyone who knows me knows I really enjoy hearing good preaching and teaching. So, it's not surprising that my customers would be quick to tell me if there was a good speaker or a new preacher in the area. In fact, a customer's recommendation had sent a friend of mine and me all the way out in the country to a little church that I would not otherwise have known existed. That night, the speaker called me out of the audience and prophesied over me. He told me that he saw expansion and that there would be many Christian bookstores in my future.

I was so excited! My heart was so full of joy and anticipation. I was so eager to see all this happen that I went home and began planning to fulfill the prophecy for the Lord. I can assure you, my trying to make the prophecy come true is not a Biblical approach at all. Looking back, I have found that a lot of problems in my life have been the result of my "helping God." I seem to easily forget that He doesn't need my help. That has been a hard lesson for me to learn. It's always been hard for me to grasp the fact that I can't work my way to heaven and that I just need to let God handle it.

This particular prophecy was one of my best efforts in the "helping God" category. *I see expansion*, that prophet had said. So, of course, it made sense to me that I would have to do something to make that happen.

Calling it a step of faith, I went to an adjoining town and found a building that I could lease. I immediately made plans to open my second store.

I had a lot of help from my staff. I had convinced them, as I had convinced myself, that this was all God's doing. My son put up the signs. My girlfriend Jody carved a wooden dove and I was ready to go. I had done it all. I had done everything...everything that is, except check with the Lord to see if this was what *He* meant by expansion. I had gotten a prophecy that I liked and I was going to make sure it was fulfilled.

What I did not know, but God did, was that one of my employees was embezzling. Because of my desire to push the prophecy forward, I now had cash registers and inventory in two different locations. The embezzler was working for himself in both of them and I was quickly going under. I had opened the second store just prior to the holiday season, which I thought would be a prime time to do so. After the season was over, I saw the error of my ways, but it was really too late to save that second store. I quickly closed it and tried to regroup.

One morning, not long thereafter, I found myself sitting at my desk with a stack of unpaid bills in front of me. Weary from trying and failing, I laid my head on my desk and cried out in desperation, "Lord, what am I doing wrong? I don't understand why I don't have the money to pay these bills. I must be buying the right products because they appear to be selling, but where is the profit?"

A young man who worked for me came up behind me as I had been praying. He put his hand on my shoulder and prayed with me, and assured me that everything was going to be all right. I didn't realize it then, but God had just given me the answer. The very person who sought to comfort me in prayer was the same person who was responsible for the problem, but at the time, I did not know it.

Fortunately, I had a very sharp store manager, Denise. She and I had discussed that something was very wrong with the store's financial picture. It was clear that product was leaving the store but the money we should have had for that product just wasn't there. We had to find out why. I had shown her how to analyze the cash register tapes and not long after our discussion, I came to work and found her sitting at the desk with a pile of cash register tapes in front of her.

"I've found it," she said triumphantly. "And I've found out who's doing it."

I sat down with her as she explained what she had discovered. There was evidence that thousands of dollars worth of product were missing with no money to show for it. Stunned, I began to add up what was unaccounted for and was astonished at the $14,000 total. No wonder the store was going under.

I called the young man in and had a private meeting with him. I showed him all the tapes on my desk and I asked him if he had anything he wanted to tell me. With the evidence in front of him, he told me that he had been stealing from me. I told him to go home and get everything that he had taken, put it in boxes, and bring it back to the store. Then we would talk again. I cannot express the sadness and disappointment I felt as he left that morning.

The next day, he came in with one cardboard box with a few things in it. I asked him to sit down. I reminded him that there was much more money missing than could be accounted for by the small amount of product he had returned.

"I want you to understand that I can forgive you, but you won't be clear unless you return *everything* that you

took. If there is so much as a pencil lying on your dresser and you know that you didn't pay for it, you need to
bring it in. This is for *your* soul, not mine," I reminded
him. "You're in school training to be a minister, so you
must understand the importance of this. I'm trying to
show you that I will forgive you, but you have to be
totally honest about what you've done."

"That's everything," he said. "That's absolutely everything."

I knew that there was more, but I didn't push him at
this meeting. I chose to wait on the Lord to show me
how to handle it this time. That very night the Lord gave
me a dream that did just that. In the dream, He showed
me that young man's bedroom in vivid detail. I had
never been in his home, let alone in his bedroom.
Clearly, God was giving me direction. The next day, I
called the boy's home. His father answered the phone. I
told him who I was and that I was calling in regards to
his son's embezzling. Then I asked him if he had gone in
his son's room and looked around.

"Oh, we don't go in his room," he replied.

"Sir, this is really quite serious. I suggest that you go
to the grocery store and get a bunch of cardboard boxes
because you are going to need them. I want you to go
and look in your son's room. Now before you object, let
me describe his room to you."

I proceeded to describe his son's bedspread, the color
of the walls, and where his dresser was placed. I
described the room in detail just as the Lord had showed
it to me in my dream. There was a brief silence on the
other end of the line before the father finally said, "Give
me time to get it together and I'll call you."

About five minutes before nine that night the boy's
father called me. He was crying as he said, "Would you
mind waiting at your store after you close and all the

employees go home so that I can bring this merchandise?"

"No problem," I told him.

When he arrived, he had a carload of boxes. There were CDs lined up side by side, two levels high. I was astounded at the amount of product he was bringing in my back door. I just sat it down on the floor in the back, overwhelmed by the enormity of it all. I looked at that distraught father and told him that I did not want his son going back to college to be a minister until he was healed. I stressed that his son needed to have counseling from their pastor and he needed a healing.

"I can't just keep him out of school," he told me.

"You really have to because he needs to work and pay back this money. I can't resell this used product and make any profit. He has to make restitution. Go home and discuss it with your family and we'll talk again."

The next morning while I was dressing for work, the Lord impressed upon me to call my manager and tell her to take the product out of the boxes that the boy's father had brought in the night before, and spread it all over the floor in the back room. *Now that's odd,* I thought. *What possible reason could there be for God telling me to do that?* Whatever His reason, I decided to be obedient. I called and Denise answered the phone.

"You're going to think I'm crazy, but the Lord's just told me to tell you to spread all that stolen product out on the floor in the back."

"No. I don't think you're crazy. If He told you to have me do it, I'll do it."

"I'll be in there shortly," I told her.

When I got to work. I walked straight to the back room. I could hardly get to my desk because the items

Denise had spread out took up most of the floor space. After picking my way through to my desk, I just sat there looking at everything on the floor. *Well, Lord, I thought. Did You want me just to see how much there is?* As I was pondering God's reason for having us create this display, there was a knock on my office door. It was the pastor of the church that this young man attended. I motioned him in and asked him to sit down in front of my desk.

"I'm here to inform you that you do not have the authority to keep this boy out of college," he stated abruptly.

I looked at him in disbelief and then stated my position clearly.

"Pastor, I want you to know that I respect pastors and I hope before you leave here, you will see my heart in this matter. I have some idea of what pastors go through, and I know how hard it is. I think that more pastors die from sheep bite than just about anything, but I want to show you my authority."

I took my right hand and I laid it on my telephone.

"Sir," I continued. "If I pick this phone up, Nationwide Insurance will come through that door within forty-eight hours. Not only will I have a check for every dime of the money that's missing, but we'll be going to court on this matter. And what this matter is, sir, is grand larceny, and it is a felony."

"You don't have the money to hire attorneys," he retorted. "You don't want to go to the expense of getting the attorneys and everything that you'll have to do."

"No sir," I interrupted, stopping him. "Evidently you don't understand insurance. I don't need to get any attorneys. That's what I pay for when I pay my insurance premium. The insurance company can get not one, not two, but three attorneys if they choose, and they will take that young man to court and they will prosecute him. Look at the floor, Pastor. What do you see?"

"I see a lot of CDs and merchandise strewn all over your floor," he answered.

"Would you be surprised if I told you that everything you see before you was stolen from me by that young man? It is no small thing. The evidence is overwhelming and the boy already confessed. I'm not the one that has a problem here. *You* do. You need to be counseling that family, and you need to let that boy know that he's not going back to school until he's healed. There are demons involved in this thing," I continued. "Have you ever seen a demon, or have you ever seen the manifestation of a demon?"

"No," he said.

"I'll tell you what. You meet me at that boy's home tonight and you'll see one. I want you to think and pray today. I want you to think and pray about what you're going to say when we get over there because I assure you, this thing is going to be settled tonight."

After agreeing to meet me that night, the boy's pastor left. I called the young man's parents, got directions to their home and told them what time we would be there. I arrived before the pastor did. The boy's parents sat on the couch. Their son sat in a chair directly across from them. I sat down in a chair on one side of the room, and when the pastor arrived, he sat across from me. The pastor began to talk to the young man about his feelings, trying to get him to express how he felt about what he had done. The young man simply said that he was sorry. Then the pastor asked him if he had ever stolen from anyone else.

The boy shook his head. "No," he replied.

247

"Stop right there," I interrupted. I called the boy by name and said, **"Face me. You foul demon of hell, if you think that I'm going to talk to you, you are wrong! I call your *lying spirit* bound right this minute in Jesus' name. You cannot utter a word. I loose this boy's tongue to speak the truth!"**

Continuing, I spoke again directly to the young man. "I say to you, the Lord showed me your room, which I've never seen and have no way of knowing what anything looked like. Yet I was able to describe it in detail to your dad. If you think God won't show me the other people you've stolen from, you are wrong. You'd better turn to your pastor and you'd better speak in your own voice, for the demon has been silenced. You had better tell him that I'm not the only one you've stolen from, and confess what you've done."

He immediately turned to his pastor and said, "I stole from my roommate at school, and I stole from all the people on the dorm floor, and I stole from the stores that were around the college and..." Unable to say more, his voice trailed off.

"Now, pastor. Can you in good conscience tell him that you still want him to go back to school?" I asked.

"No," he replied sadly. Addressing the boy, he continued, "I think it's very evident that you should not go back to school at this time."

Although the pastor left his church soon after this incident, the young man did get a healing and that night I did forgive him. I got up from my chair, knelt at his feet, put my arms around his legs, and said, "I love you and I forgive you and I want you to be healed, and I want you to know that I will never ever disclose your name. Only the employees that work for me know who you are, and I will ask them to keep your name to themselves as well."

I have seen this young man many times since that night and as far as I could tell, he really did get a healing and I believe his life has taken a better direction.

God had been faithful in showing me where a big problem was, and had shown me a way to handle the situation so people would be blessed in spite of what Satan had planned. But the ultimate failure of my store wasn't all the fault of one embezzler. I made a lot of bad decisions about the product I selected as well. But once your good product is gone, you lose your customers because they lose faith in you for not having what they really want, which is the hottest product.

There were a lot of things in play at that time. But I know now that it was God's timing for me to get out, and I really didn't have any choice. So I sold the business. My prayer as I placed it up for sale had been, "Please just let me pay all my debts," and praise God, He made it possible for me to do that. As for the young man who embezzled from my store, his father took out a loan and made restitution for what his son had stolen, and the son worked off his debt to his father. He did not go back to school at that time. So with my debts fully paid, just as I had prayed, I left that store behind. But I will always be thankful for the wonderful lessons that I learned there.

After the store was sold, the Lord moved me to Raleigh, North Carolina, where I became the District Sales Manager over four stores. There, I not only received more training, I also got a lot of lessons that would bring me closer to the completion of the tasks that the Lord has planned for me.

# Chapter
# 31

# *Ciderella—Meeting The Prince*

*L*ittle did I know that the sale of my store was a part of the "Big Plan" God had for me. As I labored at my new tasks in Raleigh, God was putting things in motion for my good.

It all started with a call from my long-time friend Bobbie. She had recently married and her husband was the rabbi of a Messianic Jewish Synagogue in Florida. She knew I had been working long hours with virtually no social life, and she was intent on helping that situation change.

"We are sending you a ticket to come stay with us. We won't take no for an answer. It goes in the mail today. You leave Tuesday, February the sixth, and will be with us through February the tenth."

One thing I can say about Bobbie is that she is always very direct and sure of herself. It certainly was a tempting offer.

"I want to come, you know I do," I began. "And the Lord knows I definitely need a rest. Let me get my schedule worked up. You had better start praying now about my claustrophobia if you want me to fly. You know that being in an enclosed place always takes me back to the attic, and even though it gets better and better every day I walk with God, I still get panicky sometimes."

"No problem," Bobbie replied, and I have no doubt that she sent that request for my peace straight to the Father as soon as she hung up the phone.

The ticket arrived and my plans were made, or so I thought. But that was before Bea called from Texas. I had known Bea for about seven years now, and I was pleased to hear from her.

"You *will* speak for me at the Atlanta show on the fifth now won't you?" she asked. "Remember, you said you would a month ago."

In all honesty, I had forgotten and now, it seemed I had a conflict. August fifth was the day before I was to leave from Raleigh for Florida.

"Yes, I do remember, Bea, but I have a problem. Friends of mine from Florida just sent me a nonrefundable ticket to stay with them a week, and I leave Raleigh on the sixth."

"No problem," she said. "You just need to get a ticket out of Raleigh to Atlanta, and then you can leave from Atlanta and go on to Florida after you speak. I have plenty of frequent flier miles if you need them. Here are the numbers to call. See what you can work out."

After Bea's call, I just sat and stared for a few minutes. It was already taking everything I had within me to talk myself into getting on to a plane for the one flight to Florida, and that would have been a straight shot. Now I had to think about Raleigh to Atlanta, and then from Atlanta to Fort Lauderdale. With my fear of flying and enclosed spaces, the thought of all this airtime was overwhelming.

Only people who are fearful of enclosures can know what this is like. I knew my Father did not give me a spirit of fear, but my days in the attic had allowed one to come on me. It didn't matter if it was an elevator or airplane. When they closed the door, my palms began to sweat, my heart raced, and my breathing became shallow. In the attic, I used to try to control my breathing. I felt that if I didn't breathe too loud, whatever lurked in the shadows would think I wasn't there.

What I needed was a way around all those plane rides. I know. I could rent a car and get my "spiritually adopted daughter" Lisa to ride to Atlanta with me. Then she could bring the car back to Raleigh and I would be back to having only one airplane ride. I had talked to myself quite a bit and I was almost comfortable with only one flight...but two? I didn't think I could do that. But with my new plan, I wouldn't have to. I breathed a sigh of relief.

Roadblocks! I hate them, don't you? Lisa couldn't go. Well, that's it. Time to face facts. Now I have to call the airlines. It was quite a relief when I found out that airline where Bea had her frequent flier mileage did *not* come through Raleigh. *That settles it,* I thought. *I tried and I can't make it work. That's it. Boy, what a relief!*

I called Bea and told her there was no way that I could get to Atlanta. I assured her that the ticket I had from Raleigh to Florida could not be changed. I really do hate to disappoint people when I have given my word, but I was sure that I had such a good excuse. With such a good reason, my conscience was really quite clear.

I think I had about an hour to enjoy my nice feeling of relief when the phone rang again. This time the call was from my dear friends, Janet and Johnny Wagoner.

"We know you are meant to speak in Atlanta. This is a true gift God has given you, and He has laid it on our hearts to make sure you get there. We have purchased a nonrefundable ticket to Atlanta. The airline that honors Bea's frequent flier miles has a flight out of Atlanta to Florida, so you are set."

Boy, do I love my nonrefundable tickets friends. They have now overridden my plan of escape.

"Lord, You are so good to me to give me such discerning friends. I'm set now, so I must move forward."

I called Barb and Jim Hickey, another couple of my friends, to see if I could stay with them in Atlanta. Although my son Joseph lives there, I knew this was not a time to visit him. Before I speak, I need solitude and I would have wanted to just enjoy being with my son. The Hickeys' home is a true sanctuary, and I would be able to prepare properly to bring God's message if I stayed there. My friends were excited and now that God had everything in place, I have to admit that I was excited. Let the trip begin!

My time with Barb and Jim was pleasant. They have been all over the world and we had been apart many times for years, but whenever we come together it is as though we lived next door all the time and had never been apart. When we find friends like this, they are true keepers. You know what I mean, like when you are fishing and you catch that really big one. That's a keeper.

It is August fifth. Today's the day I am to speak. Barb's youngest son, Kyle, has asked to go with us and hear his "Aunt Toni" speak...just a little added pressure. I really do get nervous when I speak, and if loved ones are in the audience, it seems harder. Satan loves to play little mind games with me, telling me how embarrassing it will be if I fail in front of them. However, Satan's trick didn't work this time because it did go well. It went well because I have learned to give my mouth to the Lord and step back. It is not about me. I am just the messenger.

This particular opportunity to speak was at a Christian bookstore gift show and there were many interesting people to meet. I received business cards from everyone there. At least I thought I had.

As I began to go down the staircase after speaking, two gentlemen approached the rail, each with his business card in hand. The first was a missionary from Brazil. He thanked me for the ideas I had given him that he felt would help his mission grow, and I told him I was pleased that he had found it helpful.

The second gentleman, however, owned a computer business called Resound Media. His company worked with the music industry, offering specialized computers and software for Christian retailers for their music departments. He had also been a speaker at the show. I reached for his business card and was surprised as his hands cupped mine. "Toni," he said. "I enjoyed your talk and I learned a lot, but what I really have to tell you is that I feel a connection to you."

Tears began to roll down my face, my hands still held gently between his. What was this? I don't ever remember a man's touch taking me to tears. Or could it be that it was what he had said that had gone straight to my spirit and touched me there? He released my hands and I managed to recover sufficiently to thank him and continue down the stairs. I was a little embarrassed that I had cried in front of a perfect stranger for no apparent reason, so I decided to make a quick exit.

When I reached the car where Barb and Kyle were waiting, Barb looked at me with my tear-stained face. "What's wrong?" she asked.

"I really don't know..." I began.

"I do," she interrupted. "It was that man."

"What man?" I said, all the time hoping she would answer what I already knew in my heart.

"You know. That guy with the music company. It was so obvious to everybody in the room that lightning was shooting between you two. Right, Kyle?"

"Yep," Kyle agreed.

Even Kyle had noticed! Wow! Actually, I hardly remembered looking at him, but I had to admit when he touched my hands and spoke, there was...something.

"Do you really think that?" I asked, digging for just a little more proof that something had happened, and that I wasn't imagining it.

"Yes. Yes," they both agreed.

Later that night as I was getting ready for bed, I got out all the business cards I had received that day and dumped them out on my bed. I sat cross-legged in the middle of the bed and began to sort through them. I was looking for that one special card but it wasn't there. I was going through the pile yet another time when Barb knocked on my door.

"Come in," I said.

As she opened the door, a big grin came on her face. "Looking for his card, huh?"

"Yes, I was," I admitted. "But it isn't here. I've gone through them several times and it just isn't here. Maybe there wasn't anything there after all."

"Oh, no. There was something there, all right, and you will see this man again."

"I don't know how. I didn't give him my card so he doesn't know who I am."

"He'll find you. I know he will. He'll use Bea or something. I'm telling you, he will see you again. There was too much there. Everybody saw it."

Deep inside, I hoped she was right. I left the next day for Florida.

My time in Florida was so restful and pleasant. I could sit at the rabbi's feet and learn forever. He was such a special teacher and he was able to share with me much about the Jewish roots we Christians have been grafted into. I was especially touched by the time he spoke at my church when I first met him.

I remember that he held his Bible up in the air and said, "This is a God-inspired book written by Jews about a Jew named Jesus. When it says the Gentiles are grafted in, what do you think that means? Think of it this way. If an orange tree has the limb of another tree grafted onto it, that limb becomes part of the orange tree. That limb grows to the orange tree and becomes inseparable from it. Jesus is the orange tree and you are the branches that are grafted in. Therefore, in Christ, we are one, both Jew and Gentile."

Bobbie and I have always been like sisters, but when I went to Florida it was my first opportunity to really get to know her new husband, David. I spoke to Bobbie briefly of the man I had met at the show. I remembered that his name was Rick, but I didn't know how to get in touch with him.

"If it's the Lord," Bobbie said, "He'll find you. It's time for your mate. You haven't dated in five or six years now, and we have been praying for God to send someone for you. Just be patient."

*I'm really tired of being patient,* I thought. In fact, I had been on my knees just before leaving Raleigh, begging God to make me ready. "I'm so lonely, God." I implored Him. I asked Him to do a quick work in me to finish whatever wasn't ready yet. Now if this truly is God's choice for me, He was not only listening, He was putting things in place before I even asked.

My vacation in Florida passed quickly and it was once again time to board another airplane. My trip back home was just as pleasant as the last two flights. It was great for me to be able to fly and actually talk to the people on the airplane. Usually I was a frozen block of ice, sitting motionless, but God had heard my prayer and the prayers of my friends and I had been stripped of my fear.

God's timing, as always, was perfect. Now that I was no longer a victim of the fear of flying, God could use me and he started doing just that on my flight back home from Florida. I noticed that the young man sitting next to me had a necklace with the sign of Scorpio hanging around his neck.

"Are you a Christian?" I asked him.

"Oh, yes!" he said, his face lighting up. "I've just recently given my life to the Lord. My family is very strong in the church and they've been praying for me for a long time. I had been living in Chicago, but now I'm going home a Christian and they will all be there to greet me. You can count on that!"

"That's great," I told him. "By the way, have you ever heard the story of King Saul and the fortunetellers of his land?"

"No," he answered. "But I'd like to hear it."

"Okay. Well, as you probably know, Saul was one of the kings in the Old Testament. In fact, he was king just before King David. As it happened, King Saul became involved with divination, or attempting to foresee or foretell the future. This displeased God very much because God doesn't want anyone trying to tell our future or control our lives. But here was King Saul, a leader of his people, allowing himself to be influenced by fortunetellers, astrologers, and those who practiced witchcraft.

"God convicted him of his disobedience, and Saul repented and had them all killed. As time went on, Saul's enemies began surrounding him and he found fear of the future building up inside him again. But instead of going to God with his fears, he decided to go back to the occult for answers. King Saul knew that the Scriptures warned him to 'regard not them that have familiar spirits, neither seek after wizards, to be defiled by them.' (Leviticus 19:31-KJV) But still he asked one of his servants to search the surrounding area and find a witch who could answer his questions. Upon finding a witch in the nearby province of Endor, King Saul disguised himself and went to her to seek out who would win the battle he would be facing the next day.

"This witch had the power of demon spirits in her and they showed her that the man in the disguise was, in fact, King Saul. She was terrified because she was afraid that he had come to kill her as he had the witches in his own kingdom. King Saul reassured her, telling her that she would live if she would consult a spirit for him and bring up the prophet Samuel so that he could consult with him about the future. She relented and called up Samuel for him. Samuel then told Saul that both he and his sons would die in battle the next day. And all things happened as Samuel foretold."

Then I turned to the young man, who had sat captivated as I told him the story of King Saul and the witch of Endor. "I have told you this specific story for a reason," I continued. "I noticed the necklace you wear around your neck. It has the astrological sign of Scorpio on it. You need to understand that we serve a jealous God, and He doesn't want you to be led astray by something that could hurt you. He has a very definite destiny in mind for you and it was planned long before you were born. If you ask Him, He will show you. You don't need astrology or any other device of man to show you your future. You need to let God only direct your steps."

About this time, they announced that we were about to land. A man who had been sitting on the other side of the young man had also been listening intently as I told the story about King Saul. As we fastened our seatbelts in preparation for landing, he handed the young man a tract. He never spoke and I could not see what the tract was about, but I believe that the seeds of understanding had been planted with the story, and God would use the tract, as well, to guide this young man on his Christian journey.

My friend, Bea was already at my condo when I arrived home. I had offered it to her before I left to help her defer expenses while she was in Raleigh on business. It was also my way of saying thanks for her assistance with the airfare and my speaking engagement. I had enjoyed a wonderful time, but it was definitely good to be home.

I was cooking supper for us when I began to feel sick. The next morning, I was worse.

"I won't be able to speak at your meeting today," I said. "It will be all I can do to get to work at twelve-thirty and work until nine-thirty tonight."

She seemed disappointed but accepted my reason.

"I'll see you tonight, if I make it through to nine-thirty and don't come home and go to bed first."

At work, I did not eat, hoping that by avoiding food I would be able to stay all day. I guess it was around four in the afternoon when it happened. I was in the very back of the 12,000 square foot store, showing a Bible to two ladies. You know how sometimes you feel like someone is watching you, but you haven't really seen anyone? Well, I began to have that feeling, so I looked up and there he was, just leaning against the shelves, smiling and watching me. It was the man from the Atlanta show. It was Rick!

"How long have you been there?" I asked, wondering what he had seen. My mind was racing with what kind of impression I had made, and so on.

"Are you here to see the owner?" I finally managed to say.

"Yes," he answered, still smiling. "That would be nice. But I also wanted to see you. Continue with your customers," he added.

I was suddenly a nervous wreck doing something I could usually do blindfolded. What in the world was wrong with me? I finished with my customers and told Rick I would phone the owner, as he wasn't in at the moment. I went into the back and called Irvin on his cell phone, and told him the man with Resound Media was in our store. I asked him if he would like to come back to the store and see his product.

"Sure," Irvin said. "I'll be right there."

I'd already talked with the owners, Irvin and Joanna, about Rick's company's product. I had primed Irvin on what a great system for ordering music and customer service the system was. After going back out front, I found Rick standing in the gift department with a lovely blonde haired lady.

"I have a place for you to set up your computers," I informed him. "If you'll follow me, I'll show you." As we walked away, the lady did not come with us, so I said, "Why didn't you introduce me to your wife?" I asked, trying to sound more casual than I felt.

"Oh, I'm not married," he said, rather matter-of-factly.

I was a few steps ahead of Rick with my back to him so he didn't see the big smile that came on my face. I was so glad that he was behind me because that smile would have been a dead giveaway to my pleasure at his answer.

I showed him where to set up and left when Irvin came in. But after the demonstration, I walked over to see how it went.

"Well, are we getting this system?" I asked Irvin. Irvin is a witty man and he just loves to pull my chain.

"Yep, we sure are," he said. "I worked a real deal. We're getting them in all four stores and I'm trading *you* for all of them."

My face turned crimson and this time, there was no hiding it from Rick.

"Great," Rick said. "I've been trying to figure out how I could get her to Washington State. It sounds like a fantastic deal to me!"

Just as he was asking me if I got a dinner break, Bea walked up.

"Oh, Rick," she said. "How wonderful to run into you. I was hoping we could have dinner together."

Rick gave me a questioning look.

"That's fine with me," I said, thinking it might actually be a little easier to talk. Well, as it turned out, we were all able to talk, but we didn't talk about the things I had hoped. I left that dinner knowing nothing more about this fascinating man than I had before. After dinner, Rick and I again said goodbye as we had in Atlanta. There were no tears this time, just a tearing-away feeling inside...a feeling of unfinished business.

That night Bea asked, "What's this with you and Rick?"

"Not anything that I know of," I said.

"Oh, there's more there than meets the eye," she said. "You two will be an item soon."

"Do you really think so?" I questioned, hoping that she was right.

"Definitely," she said.

Bea left the next morning and I was off to work. At nine-thirty, before the store opened, they announced over the speaker, "Toni, line one is for you."

"Hello. This is Toni," I said.

"Hi, Toni. This is Rick."

My heart leapt and I had to struggle not to drop the phone.

"I'm sorry to call you at work, but I had no other way to reach you."

"That's okay," I said, trying not to let him hear that I was out of breath, my heart was beating so hard. "What can I do for you?" I asked, trying to sound professional.

"I just have one question and I hope I'm not being rude, but I know no other way to get past this. Are you married?"

"Married?" I repeated, totally unprepared for that question. "Why no, and I wouldn't have gone to dinner with you if I had been married."

"Well, I had to be sure. I did see a diamond on your hand, but I didn't want to stare."

"That was my middle finger," I said.

"Then may I call you at home?

"I would love that," I responded, still trying to calm my racing heart. "Here's my number."

"Thank you. I'll call this evening. Have a good day."

"You, too," I said. I held the phone for several seconds after he hung up, as I was still too stunned to put it down. The rest of the day I was flying high. Finally it was closing time, and I could hardly wait to get home.

I quickly went upstairs to count the money and prepare the cash drawer for our day. As I sat at the desk, Irvin came through the door, put a hammerlock on my head and said, "This guy is it! Everyone can see that there's something between you two and if you mess this up, I'll kick your butt."

"Oh, Irvin," I protested. "I hardly know him. How can you say that?"

"Because it's obvious. You'll see. It's there for anyone with eyes to perceive. But you had better be good. This is a good man."

The phone call that night was unlike any I had ever had. Rick and I talked for two hours like we had known each other for years. We had so much in common. Neither of us had met our real father. We both had very strong good father figures, whom we loved very much. We liked the same music, the same food, and the same fun things to do. It was awesome. But most of all, we shared the same faith. As we started to wind down, Rick surprised me with another first.

"Toni," he said. "I may blow it right here but I'm going to say it anyway. I have not dated in over twelve years and this is unlike me. But I'm in love with you, and I feel the Lord has already told me you will be my wife."

I wanted so to say the same thing back, but I couldn't quite get those exact words out so I said that I did feel this was of the Lord and reassured him. "No," I said, "You haven't blown it. To the contrary, I love your honesty. But you *do* remember starting this conversation with 'I want to go slow,' don't you, Rick?"

We both laughed. What a beginning!

Isn't it like that when we meet the Lord for the first time? We're flying with angels' wings in heavenly places. No wonder He keeps calling us back to our First Love. He wants us to reconnect at that fresh untouched spot in us that totally surrenders to the moment when He looked us in the eyes and said, "Right where you are. Right this minute. I know we are connected," and you know that you know that you know that He is right. Then the journey begins as you begin to incorporate your friends and family with your new Love.

# Chapter
## 32

# Prince Or Frog?

*I*t would be some time before I would see Rick again, but we talked two or more hours on the phone every day, so we were more than ready to see each other when Rick came back to Raleigh on the third of March. We were both looking forward to being together again, and although it was a good reunion, it did feel surprisingly awkward. You would think it would have been a piece of cake with all the talking we had done by phone and e-mail over the last few months, but walking your talk is not as easy as it looks. There still seemed to be a lot of things that needed to be put in place...or were there?

Maybe that's where we start going wrong spiritually, as well. If the Lord is willing to come to us right where we are, why should we have to rearrange ourselves so all the good and perfect stuff we think we have to show Him is up front? He bore us in the Spirit, after all, and His Spirit is all-knowing. Oh, but I was talking about human love, wasn't I? You know, the kind where you always try to put your best foot forward.

The first three meals I cooked for Rick were burned, bland, dried-out and hard to chew. So, I wasn't exactly coming out of the chute strong, if you know what I mean. To everyone who knows me well, I am known as "the cook and entertainer." I love to have people into my home and I love cooking for them. They usually rave about the dishes I serve and often ask for recipes. But you would probably have had a hard time convincing Rick of that in the beginning.

With Rick living on the West Coast and my living on the East Coast, we never really were able to get into a normal dating pattern, and I think all those steps are so important in building a relationship. Unfortunately, we missed out on that. Rick would come in to Raleigh every four weeks or so. I would cook. We would rent movies and spend time together, but we were never out with other people, interacting as a couple. The time we had together always seemed so short that we didn't really have time to plan get-togethers with friends. So we spent our precious time with each other, thinking that was the most important part.

Now I see that while time with just the two of us was and is very important, we were missing a very strategic part of building a relationship. I should have remembered the spiritual parallel. When you first begin your relationship with Jesus, you need Christian friends to challenge the best in you. I remember hearing a famous golfer once say that he would always play with someone who would stretch his game. And that is exactly what Rick and I did not do. We did not stretch our relationship.

Expanding your horizons to include time with other couples allows you to see another side of your man. You get to see what he is like when he is talking and relating to your girlfriend or her husband or boyfriend. It is also very important to see how he relates to another man and he should have the benefit of seeing how you relate to others, as well. This essential building block was very definitely missing from the foundation of our relationship. Regardless of what may have been missing, we chose not to see it at that time. In fact, it wasn't long before Rick got down on his knees with an engagement ring in his hands, and asked me to be his wife. Of course, I said yes.

As the months passed, Rick decided, much to my delight, to move to North Carolina and establish a satellite office. His business was operating out of Seattle, Washington at that time, and the cross-country trips were beginning to wear on both of us. So in July, 2001, Rick began preparation to move east. Shortly after Rick arrived, we began looking for a house to buy. We wanted our new married life to have brand new surroundings for both of us. We found a house on a lake with the most serene setting. I was sure that everything was fitting together so perfectly.

At the same time we were buying the house, I was knee-deep in wedding preparations. We had set our date as September ninth, 2001. The condo I was currently living in was for sale and the realtor had people marching in and out every day. I was frantically trying to keep everything looking perfect all the time.

At this point, things were beginning to weigh heavily on both Rick and me and the pressure just kept building. In the midst of everything else, I received a call from my brother asking me to come back home to Arkansas, as our dad was not doing well. Even though the wedding invitations needed to be in the mail, we left for Arkansas.

I was glad to have my family meet Rick, and they all welcomed him with open arms. I stayed mostly at my dad's side, leaving Rick alone in his motel room much of the time. But he didn't complain. I really appreciated his sacrifice. I truly believed that I was probably spending the last moments I would have with my dad. But once again, Rick and I found ourselves in rather unusual circumstances. We tried to make the best of it and still continue building our relationship. Much to my surprise and delight, my dad began to rally some, and we felt that it would be reasonable to leave and go back to Raleigh.

Once we were back in North Carolina, the race was on. The wedding was now only six weeks away. My job was requiring some extra-long days, and I found that I could not find the energy or the time to do all that I had to do. I'm not sure if this is where "the monster" entered or if it was lurking within me even before this. What I do know is that when I shifted into high gear, I entered another level of existence–and it was an awful place. I found no peace and everything around me seemed to move in slow motion.

Rick was out at our new home, busily painting the walls and preparing the house for me to move in. My condo had been sold and I would have to move out just before the wedding. For me, moving is a horrendous job. I have been a pack rat for years, but there was no time to sort through all that stuff now. We would just have to move it. I saw that Rick was working very hard to get everything in place so we could come back from our honeymoon to a home that was basically settled, but by now, the monster within me had taken over. I was so far up in the emotional ozone that I didn't want to see that my bridegroom needed some loving kindness. Instead he received Sergeant Toni's daily duty roster.

Do you think it's like that with the Lord? I think it often is. Our Heavenly Bridegroom has wooed us to Him and we've reached our first plateau of communication, and everything in the relationship is so blissful. It's then that the monster of "I am so busy, Lord" takes over. "Just hang on, Lord," we say. "I have such plans for us. Just as soon as I build this dream world I've got going here, I'll be right back to get You."

Have we left our first love? Oh, yes. That is exactly what we have done. And that is what I was doing to Rick. He did not complain, so I thought he would be okay. But the Lord doesn't complain either, you know. You've heard people say that they wonder where the Lord went while they were busy "doing their own thing." Well, He hasn't moved. He's back there where you left Him. Just waiting. So was Rick.

The wedding I had planned was so elaborate. My gown was custom-designed and hand-made. The head-piece and bouquet were a gift from my girlfriend Judy and were a true labor of love. Judy is a jewelry design-er and she stayed up until two in the morning finishing the headpiece one weekend before the wedding, despite the fact that she was experiencing physical and emotion-al trauma at the time. She had just been diagnosed with a cluster of tumors at the base of her skull in the spinal column, yet she gave to me of her time and effort in spite of her own circumstances. I had tried to convince her that this sacrifice was not necessary and that I could get another headpiece, but she was determined to com-plete it.

"The Lord sent you here just for this purpose," she told me, as we sat together at her home. "He gave me this talent and it is helping me that we can pray and work together."

She was ready to proceed with such determination and love. How could I refuse her gift? So we worked together and prayed diligently. By the end of our week-end together, the exquisite headpiece was finished. Not only was it beautiful to look at, it had so much love in it that it took my breath away.

One week later Judy had surgery to have the tumors removed. The pathology results confirmed that the tumors were benign. Praise God for His healing power!

The events planned around the wedding included a pig picking for the out-of-town guests and a pre-wedding party. My son Joseph and his roommates, Bill and Johnny, pulled a cooker all the way from Atlanta. They cooked the pig, together with a big vat of Brunswick stew and all the trimmings the night before the pig pick-ing.

Two days before the wedding, Rick's friends from Seattle arrived. Affectionately known as the Delta Force, Rick and his friends were a tight-knit group and the night they arrived was quite a night! Joseph and Johnny had been cooking a special meal for Rick and me, but rushed out to purchase more groceries when they found out Rick's best man Jeff, and his friends, Tim and Jerry, were arriving from Seattle. As for me, I was still running on high octane and was out shopping for last minute wedding stuff, so I didn't get home until just an hour before Rick and the Delta Force were due to arrive for dinner.

"Quick, Mom. Go freshen up," Joseph said as I entered the front door. "Rick's friends will be here in one hour. We're cooking a fabulous meal for them and we've got everything under control here, so you go do your thing."

Rick arrived just as I was putting the finishing touches to my hair and makeup. By the time I came out to greet the guests, it seemed that Joseph and Johnny had stolen the show. The dinner was sensational and everyone was quite cordial. But as you now know, Joseph is gay and meeting him and his friend Johnny was a new experience for Rick's friends, so the questions flew. By two o'clock in the morning, I was zonked and excused myself to retire. I tried to get Joseph to go to bed, as well, because I figured he would probably scare the pants off Rick and his Delta Force with some of our family stories. But no, it was not to be. Unbeknownst to me, there was a true plan unfolding.

The pig picking was the next night. It was held at the home of my friends Johnny and Janet. Barb and Jim Hickey had come in from Atlanta and together with Johnny and Janet they transformed the spacious yard into a paradise. A big yellow-striped tent had been erected near the shore of the gorgeous lake, which skirts their property. The entire area was awash with candlelight, festive bows, and beautiful flowers. The setting could not have been more perfect for a pre-wedding celebration. It should have been a grand event but some things that we had not planned were about to happen.

I arrived early and I was overwhelmed at all my friends had done. I was just beginning to take everything in when my cousin Steve approached me.

"Let's go for a quick ride," he said. "I need to talk to you privately."

I excused myself from Johnny and Janet, explaining I would be right back, and joined my cousin in Johnny's truck. Steve had come in from Alaska for my wedding and I was very glad to see him, but I wondered what could possibly be so important that he would ask me to leave my party, even for a brief time. But I was soon to find out. What he had to say stung me very deeply and I felt like the paralyzed victim of a spider, knowing that I was soon to be devoured.

"I didn't come all the way here from Alaska to be the only family member to put a damper on your wedding," he began. "But I am here to protect you. And Toni, I see red flags. You are free to do what you want with this information, but know that I care about you and your future and I know your dad would want me to tell you."

As he began to tell me his story, I felt as if my whole world was crumbling around me. Apparently, Rick's friends had chosen the same motel in which to stay as had my cousin. They were all sitting around the motel's refreshing pool, talking about the upcoming wedding. They had not met my cousin Steve, so their conversation flowed freely even though he could easily overhear all they had to say. They were discussing my gay son Joseph, their friend Rick and his business, plus a few other tidbits that had my cousin quite concerned. As we rode in the truck, Steve shared the conversations and his concerns with me.

271

We arrived back at the pig picking and I got out of the truck. I felt shell-shocked. I began walking around among the guests, but mentally, I was somewhere else. While I made a pretense of mingling with my guests, my mind went over and over the information I had just received from my cousin. I was still trying to sort it all out in my mind when a sweet new friend named Carla took my hand and said, "You're coming with me."

There was no room for argument given the tone of Carla's voice, so I went with her. She led me down to the water's edge a short distance away from the party site. There was a John boat with a trolling motor tied to the pier.

"Get in," she said. "We're having a little talk." With that, she started the motor and out on the water we went. "Now you know I'm planning on getting married in just a few weeks," she said, "which gives me some insight into what I see. Let me tell you this, Toni. If I have a look on my face the day before my wedding like you have on yours right now, I want you to put me in this boat and drown me in this lake. Something is not right. Where is your fiancé?"

"He's gone to Raleigh to pick up his tux," I said defensively. "He forgot to get it yesterday."

"Well, when he gets here, I'll put him in this boat and tell him the same thing I'm telling you. Something is very wrong here. Your friends love you. They have all rallied to give you your dream wedding. But more than that, Toni, we all want you to be happy."

Carla was confirming doubts that had been swirling about in my mind for several days and I thanked her for being so frank with me.

"You are absolutely right," I agreed "There's more going on here than I can deal with alone. As soon as Rick gets here, I will settle it...whatever it is."

About that time Carla pulled the boat back up to the shore and we climbed out, David, the rabbi who was to perform our marriage ceremony, walked up to us. He and his wife, Bobbie, had flown in from Florida.

"As soon as Rick gets here, I want him to come to this boat. I want to talk to you both. But I can tell you right up front, Toni. I will not marry you tomorrow. Not the way things are."

He had no more finished speaking when Rick and the rabbi's wife Bobbie walked over to the place where I was standing.

"Talk," the Rabbi said. "We will stand over here so no one can get by us to interrupt you two."

I told Rick what the Rabbi had said about not marrying us. I explained to Rick that I did not understand his recent actions, either at rehearsal where he appeared distant and cold, or his forgetting the tux and arriving late for our party.

"Toni," he began. "I love you but I just can't handle you. We need more time."

I was furious. "So what do you think will be different with more time? Do you think I will change? I'm me. This is it. What you see is what you get!"

"It's me I'm worried about, Toni. I can't say no to you, and we won't last six months with you running the show." Then his voice softened and he said, "The Rabbi has suggested that we tell everyone this is an engagement party and we're deciding to postpone the wedding. I think we should take his advice."

Reluctantly, I agreed.

When we got back to the party area, the Rabbi called us up to the microphone. Did I mention we had a band? When I walked up to the bandstand with Rick, I just stood with him as he held my dishrag-limp hand while the Rabbi made the announcement

"God is good," he began. "And God is still in charge."

After he had told the crowd about the decision to postpone the wedding, I was so numb that I don't remember much about what was said. Everyone began to come up and hug our necks, and tell us they were proud of our strength. I know they were trying to be encouraging, but I remember thinking, *what strength*? In my mind, instead of the fireworks that were supposed to go off over the lake that night, I saw my dream exploding.

I finally made it into the house, and was preparing to gather up my things when my eyes caught sight of the groom's cake, which had been placed on a nearby table. The cake had been made in the shape of a knight in shining armor. It also represented a man with God's armor, His sword, His helmet and His breastplate...the works. I was stunned to see that someone had taken the sword and cut his head off. *I guess one of my friends is as mad as I am*, I thought.

Johnny and Janet came up to me and Johnny pressed a one hundred dollar bill into my hand.

"Get a room at a hotel in town," he instructed. "Don't try to drive back to Raleigh tonight."

Another hand touched my arm and I looked down into eyes that were confused, yet full of love. For the first time since everything had happened, I realized that I had my precious granddaughter beside me. The beautiful love story that I had wanted to unfold in front of her had quickly turned into a nightmare. She was only eight years old, but what an incredible child. She was actually consoling me.

I took her with me to the motel and the next morning, I let her go to the lobby to get anything she wanted to eat at the buffet. She came back with lots of goodies and announced, "Rick was there eating."

I asked her to go tell him to call me since I did not know what room he was in. Not long afterward the phone rang. It was Rick. I asked him how he thought I was supposed to get through this mess. What was I supposed to do with the house we were purchasing? I certainly could not afford it on my salary alone. He quickly tried to reassure me.

"I will be making the house payment for as long as needed until we have a chance to work things out. I love you, Toni. Nothing about that has changed. I just need to find the man in me."

I did not say I loved him or that I intended to work on anything. I was a seething volcano inside, and much too angry to think about working things out. All I could think of was how many times in my life was I going to be rejected and still have any of me left?

Oh, the plans God has for us. They are so awesome but we seldom see them in His light. I certainly was not seeing anything of God's great plan right then from my limited viewpoint.

I drove home to Raleigh after dropping my grand-daughter Aryn off at her mom's. When I walked in the door of our new home, it all hit me. We had been working on this house, putting things in place so that it would not be such a chore after the honeymoon. Now, as I looked around at the newly painted cabinets and walls, I was crumbling inside and I began to cry. Suddenly the phone rang, startling me. Despite my tears, I answered. It was Joseph and as soon as I heard his voice, I became a sobbing mess.

"I knew it, Mom," Joseph said. "I knew you would be all to pieces. Please get yourself together and come to the beach. We will wait on you hand and foot and show you the time of your life."

As I considered his offer, I heard a knocking sound.

"Hold on, Joe. Someone is knocking at my door. I can't imagine anyone knowing I am here. After all, it is supposed to be my wedding day."

I opened my door and was surprised to look into the beautiful face of my son Bryan's godmother, Sherry Heilig.

"How in the world did you find me?" I asked.

"I have MapQuest® in my car. Grab something to sleep in and a toothbrush. I have a room for us. You are not spending your wedding night in this house under these circumstances. From the looks of you, you have been in here too long already."

"Oh, my goodness!" I exclaimed. "I still have Joseph on the phone." Grabbing the receiver, I asked, "Son, have you been listening? It's your Aunt Sherry."

"Thank God," Joe said. "I am so glad, Mom. She is just what the doctor ordered. I know you will be okay now. Try and have fun."

With Sherry at my side, having fun might just be a possibility, despite the day's dark shadows. Our friendship had always been so spontaneous and genuine. It seemed that we always just picked up where we left off the last time we were together.

I will never forget the day we met. It was a lawn party for the Commander's wife of our husbands' Squadron. I was still married to Brad then and Sherry and her husband had just arrived on base. This party was her first official function. I was well entrenched in the Officers'

Wives' Club, with my newest project being a school for retarded children. What first caught my attention was Sherry's beautiful long black hair, but I wanted to see if there was more to her than just surface beauty.

"Hi! My name is Toni," I said, by way of introduction. "When you're finished getting your plate, would you like to sit with us? I will be at that table over there." I continued. She smiled and those crystal blue eyes just twinkled. I liked her immediately. Well, that is, until she began to talk.

She started telling us all about her being an airline stewardess working out of Texas. Fascinated at her occupation, the other wives asked her about some of her experiences. It was then that she began to share one of her most "horrifying" experiences. She had been on a plane that had to make an emergency landing. The emergency landing wasn't as bad as this gosh-awful burg of a town called Blytheville, Arkansas, where they had been forced to set the plane down, she told us. As she rambled on about how tiny and "hicksville" this place was, I finally interrupted.

"Sherry, do you remember who invited you to sit here with us?"

Now I had her attention.

"Oh, no-o-o," she said. "Not in a million years."

"Yep," I said, confirming her worst fears. "I was born and raised in Blytheville, Arkansas."

From that day, I knew we were destined to be lifelong friends. Now here she stood, ready to help me heal. And we did have fun, just as Joseph had hoped we would. But all too soon she had to head back to Florida. With promises to see each other soon, we parted and as I walked back in my house, I knew that it was better but it was not over.

# Chapter
## 33

# *The True Bride*

*I*t was now September the eleventh. Just two short days after I was to have been married, the World Trade Center and the Pentagon were attacked by terrorists, destroying the Twin Towers and heavily damaging the Pentagon. I sat with the rest of the nation in horrified numbness, watching the ongoing news coverage.

Rick had gone to Baja, Mexico, Sunday evening to try to sort things out. His friend Pastor Tim had left him there with the intention of going back to pick him up, but with all our nation's borders closed and all the planes grounded, Rick was stranded.

The sadness I felt over the attacks was overwhelming. I chided myself on how could I be hurting over a little ol' wedding when so many people had lost their lives, and the whole world seemed to be crashing in on the loved ones left behind. Like many others in our nation that day, I knew it was time to talk to God.

"Is this the end of my story, Lord? Have I missed something?

**"You are not the bride I am coming back for."** The voice was all too familiar.

"What do you mean, Father?"

**"My bride will be attentive. Her eyes will be totally on me. Search your heart."**

I did and all I saw were desires for the perfect wedding. God was doing a personal work in me in the midst of one of the world's greatest tragedies.

When I am on the Potter's wheel, I can feel it when He stops the wheel from spinning. There is a long straw-like instrument that a potter picks up to dislodge an imperfection in the clay. Stopping the wheel, he digs into the pot for that imperfection that his sensitive fingers detected as the clay was spinning. Ever so gently, he flicks the imperfection out and resumes working on his creation. I knew in my spirit that the wheel had stopped.

The spirit of perfection I had embraced since childhood was about to be confronted by my Lord, but was I ready? Did this mean He would strip me of my spontaneity and zeal for projects? Would there be nothing left? I wondered, but I held still on the wheel, letting the Potter flick away. For there is one thing I knew then and I know now. We serve a balanced God. When He takes away, He replenishes.

As soon as what was to have been my honeymoon week's vacation was up, I was back at work. Everyone was very quiet about the wedding that did not happen. I had been back working at the store about a month when Irvin called me into his office. He reluctantly informed me that I would need to look for another job as they would be laying off many employees, and possibly even closing two of their stores. I certainly understood that there weren't funds for management level salaries such as mine, and starting the cuts there was a logical business step.

I was given thirty days' notice, and at first I wasn't too concerned about looking for another job. But I soon discovered that my salary range was a drawback that made finding a new job quite difficult. I quickly began to find new meaning in the word humble. Still, I never lost sight of all I had to be thankful for. I was living in a beautiful home on a lake and Rick was paying the mortgage.

I thought that perhaps a roommate could help me cover my bills until I got another job, so I put an ad in the paper. I never got even one response. What I really needed was to see what Rick was going to turn into. After all, he had said he was going to become a man who could not only take care of me but "handle me" as well. I really knew that he had seen the worst that I could become when I micromanaged our wedding and ignored him.

Well, I surely didn't have much to manage now, and in another four weeks when my job actually ended, I would have even less. I found out very quickly that the job market was dead, and the aftermath of September 11th loomed in the air with a daily gloom as story after story aired on TV and radio. I wondered if joy was ever going to come back to our nation...or back to me.

The holiday season began, and it helped to think of family and select gifts to surprise them and put smiles on their faces. Now that I was not working, I had time to cook, which I had not been able to do for years. Rick came to Raleigh for Christmas, even though he had moved his things back to Seattle back in October. We had talked through a lot of things, but I was not over the loss of my dream wedding that I felt I had waited a lifetime for.

I did start to see Rick taking more control of what we would and would not do. But with my job loss and the derailed wedding, I was broken to the point where my spirit was like a wet noodle. For the first time, I think I looked at brokenness in its totality. It encompassed me.

I think it was after Christmas that Rick saw that we weren't going to build any bridges for healing as long as he stayed in Seattle. He felt he needed to be in North

Carolina. He was so right. So in January, we discussed a new plan. Rick would move back and store his things back in the garage. When he wasn't on the road for his job, he would stay in a motel up the street.

Now that he was closer, our talks were good, but I don't think that there was any big catalyst or anything like that that happened. Rick and I needed time to sort through how we wanted our marriage structured, and what our boundaries would be. I acknowledged my anger at him and the Delta Force. But now, with the benefit of hindsight, I was so thankful for all that had transpired. I knew that Rick's friends had been used by God to make Rick and me take a closer look at ourselves and our relationship.

For me, I believe God wanted to know if I wanted a big wedding or a good man–and what if I couldn't have either one? It was like Abraham being asked to put Isaac on the altar. Abraham couldn't take a sacrifice up the mountain, but would he sacrifice his son when he got there. What God wanted to know was, *will you give it all up and still love just Me*? I surrendered. "Yes, Lord," I said. "If I can't have a big wedding, and even if I have to give up my husband-to-be, I will always love You."

Finally I was able to relinquish all thoughts of my "dream wedding" and let forgiveness fill my heart. I was finally prepared to let it all go.

Remember when I said that God loves surprises. Well, I was about to be reminded of this myself in a very special way. I got another phone call from Rabbi Barsky and his wife Bobbie.

"Have you set a new wedding date?" they asked.

"March ninth," I answered.

"Great!" said Bobbie. "Here's the deal. You and Rick come to Florida. David will do the entire service. Your reception party and your honeymoon suite in the Radisson Resort are all on us. We will have everything prepared when you arrive and I will break your legs if you try to help in any way. Just be the radiant bride and let us wait on you. We have a praise team at church so just let us know what songs you would like. Invite whoever you want."

I hung up the phone in disbelief. Rick and I made plans to go to Florida.

Our wedding day was so blessed. The weather was perfect and the members of Rabbi Barsky's church who attended were so precious. Our friends from Atlanta flew in. Colonel Jim Hickey gave me away, and his wife Barb did everything to help Bobbie and the chef.

I had just surrendered my "dream wedding" to the Lord and He had just given it back to me–and I had to do nothing but receive it. In the sight of God and all present, I was the beloved bride.

# Epilogue

## The End...Or The Beginning?

Now I ask you. WHERE ARE YOU GOING?! It doesn't matter to God where you have been. If it did, He would never have used Mary Magdalene, Paul, David, Jacob, or Moses and many more. They were not perfect. I am a flawed person also, but I know and acknowledge the times in my life that I have been broken. Brokenness is so vital to our walk with the Lord. Let's look at the beginning of man as described by one of my favorite authors, Don Nori, in his book *The Power of Brokenness*. God has just created man, as Brokenness stands by watching and wondering what part she is to play in this new creation. Listen to her thoughts:

"She saw that man had been especially designed to experience union with God Himself. He was created uniquely incomplete, as it were, for his destiny was dependent upon his dependency. This design of dependency was not from a morbid compulsion for control, but from God's eternal longing for union, for partnership.

As Brokenness watched the man embrace his Creator Father, she also came to understand the gravity of her own existence and exactly what it was that the Father expected. As that thought gripped her heart, the Father turned slightly so that His eyes would catch her gaze. He knows, she thought to herself. He knows that I am finally understanding.

Brokenness walked slowly to her Lord's side. 'You have begotten me to serve You, and serve You I will.' Then as the Lord smiled, she turned and walked away.

Brokenness was consumed with thought. She pondered what the millennia would bring as she befriended each generation of humanity. Will they listen to me? Will they understand the importance of my friendship? Will they welcome me as the companion the Father intends me to be? Or will they merely consider me an intrusion upon their plans, a stumbling block to their dreams and aspirations, and a thorn that intrudes upon their comfort?

Suddenly Brokenness realized that the Lord was standing in front of her. Startled by His abrupt appearance, she embraced Him and wept on His shoulder. He spoke softly. 'Their greatest asset is also their greatest liability.' He paused for a moment, giving Brokenness time to understand His words. 'Yes, I know how powerful they will feel as they exercise their option to choose their own destiny, but the power to choose is the very glory of My relationship with them. They must choose to serve Me. They must choose to love Me. Without this risk, without this choice, there can never be true love, true union, or true devotion to anything. But you My dear, dear Brokenness, will be their secret weapon. You will be their hope. For only you can convince them to come to Me. Only you can convince them to relinquish their will to Mine and their dreams to My dreams. You alone can convince them to trust Me implicitly. You will show them mercy and bring them conviction, hope, repentance, and deliverance.'"

Now I ask you again. WHERE ARE YOU GOING? Would you like to go on an adventure? It's really as simple as that! Ask the One Who created you to lead you to your purpose. He will lead you everywhere you need to be and give you many surprises along the way. "My children have not because they ask not," He says. "And then when they do ask they ask for the wrong thing." Ask for His will in your life. It's always the best choice.

# From The Author

I would like to acknowledge the following authors and their books, for they have truly played a big part in my healing, and I am listing them in the order in which I read them:

*The Holy Bible – King James Version*

*The Problem With Doing Your Own Thing* – Bob Mumford, Elim Publishing.

*Telling Yourself The Truth* – William Backus and Marie Chapian, Bethany House (February 2000) ISBN: 0764223259.

*Healing for Damaged Emotions* – David Seamands, Chariot Victor Books (October 1991) ISBN: 0896939383.

*Me and My Big Mouth: Your Answer Is Right Under Your Nose* – Joyce Meyer Warner Books (October 2002) ISBN: 0446691070.

*Boundaries* – Henry Cloud, John Townsend, Zondervan (April 2002) ISBN: 0310247454.

*The Three Battle Grounds* – Dr. Francis Frangipane, Destiny Image Abridged edition (February 2003) ISBN: 0768402166.

*Prayer and Fasting* – Dr. Kingsley Fletcher, Whitaker House (January 1999) ISBN: 0883685434.

*Break the Generation Curse* – Marilyn Hickey, Marilyn Hickey Ministry (1998) ISBN: 1564410048.

*The Power of Brokenness* (Re-released as *Tales of Brokenness*) – Don Nori, Destiny Image (October 2002) ISBN: 0768420741.